WITCHES IN OLD NORTH YORKSHIRE

by
Mary Williams

HUTTON PRESS

1987

Published by the Hutton Press Ltd.
130 Canada Drive, Cherry Burton, Beverley
East Yorkshire HU17 7SB

Copyright © 1987

First Published 1987
Reprinted 1992

Printed by Clifford Ward & Co.
(Bridlington) Ltd.
55 West Street, Bridlington, East Yorkshire
YO15 3DZ

ISBN 0 907033 54 7

CONTENTS

ACKNOWLEDGEMENTS

The Author wishes to thank the following persons for so kindly assisting her in the preparation of this book:

Mr. Larry Bruce, Reference Librarian at Cleveland County Libraries, for his help in organising the photographs of material in the County's Local Collection.

Mr. D. Tyrell and the staff of the Cleveland County Records Office.

Mr. Ashcroft and the staff of the North Yorkshire Records Office.

The Whitby Museum and the Whitby Literary and Philosophical Society.

The staff of Middlesbrough Central Reference Library.

Miss Doyle and Mrs. Booth of the Redcar Reference Library.

Whitby Gazette.

Mr. D. Smith and the staff of the Ryedale Folk Museum.

Mr. B. Frank, MBE, the Founder of the Ryedale Folk Museum.

Mr. C. Scott-Wilson, writer and local historian.

Mr. T. Middlemass of the University of Durham.

INTRODUCTION

In this age of high technology, space travel and the like, there seems to be a growing interest in things that happened in the past. Perhaps it is a reaction against too much technology. Perhaps it comes from an uneasy feeling that we still don't know everything about the world around us and we find it comforting to look back at the days when our ancestors knew even less.

Whatever the reason, witchcraft is one feature of our past history that fascinates a great many of us. There are so many questions to be answered. What were these strange, uncanny witches really like? Had they really powers beyond those of their fellow men? If not, why were so many of their neighbours convinced that they had?

Some historians believe that witchcraft had its roots in a pre-Christian religion. Did witches earn their sinister reputation because they practised ancient rituals disapproved of by the Christian Church? When they leapt about dressed in animal skins, each with a broomstick between her knees — to make the crops grow — did these antics lead to stories that they could turn themselves into animals, could ride across the night sky on a broomstick? Such stories were current, and really believed, less than a century ago.

The North Yorkshire witches, male and female, well-meaning or evilly-intentioned, that you will find in this book have been arranged geographically, according to the part of Yorkshire where they are believed to have lived. They can also be divided historically into two groups. There are those who lived in the days when witchcraft was a punishable offence by English Law, and these have come to light by the aid of Court Records. There are also those who were believed to have operated after the laws against witchcraft were repealed in 1736 (you cannot change people's beliefs by Act of Parliament).

The latter group don't, of course, appear as witches in official records. Fortunately, towards the end of the 19th century, we had in North Yorkshire two very enthusiastic 'witch-hunters' amongst our local historians — Richard Blakeborough of Guisborough (1850-1918) and Canon John C. Atkinson of Danby (1814-1900). Each went round country districts gathering stories from senior citizens about local witches who had been around in their lifetimes or whose stories had been handed down to them from previous generations. Had these not been recorded, they would have been lost for ever when the tellers of such tales were, one by one, laid to rest in North Yorkshire graveyards.

Using modern family-history research techniques it has been possible, in some cases, to identify a supposed witch as an actual person, adding authentic detail to what Blakeborough and Atkinson recorded. It is hoped that this will provide an even clearer picture of these uncanny creatures who plagued (or occasionally helped) our great-great-grandparents in the late 18th and early 19th century.

You will not find any scientific explanations of the supernatural happenings produced by these North Yorkshire witches of ours. You will find speculations here and there. It is up to you whether to accept these speculations as explanations or not...

MARY WILLIAMS
Marske, Redcar
May 1987

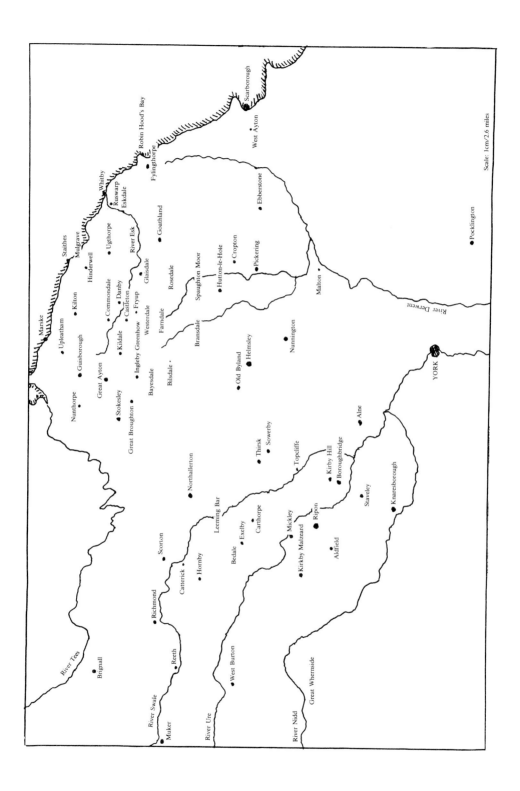

Scale: 1cm/2.6 miles

Scarborough

Robin Hood's Bay

West Ayton

Fylingthorpe

Whitby
Ruswarp
Eskdale

Ebberstone

Goathland

River Esk

Pocklington

Staithes
Mulgrave
Hinderwell
Ugthorpe
Commondale
Danby
Castleton
Glaisdale

Rosedale

Cropton
Hutton-le-Hole
Pickering

Marske
Upleatham
Kilton
Guisborough
Kildale
Fryup
Westerdale
Farndale

Spaughton Moor

Malton

River Derwent

Nunthorpe
Great Ayton
Ingleby Greenhow
Bayesdale
Bilsdale

Bransdale

Old Byland
Helmsley

Nunnington

YORK

Stokesley
Great Broughton

Alne

Thirsk
Sowerby

Northallerton

Topcliffe
Kirby Hill
Boroughbridge

Leeming Bar

Knaresborough
Staveley

Scorton

Bedale
Exelby
Carthorpe
Mickley
Ripon
Aldfield

Catterick
Hornby

Kirkby Malzeard

Richmond

River Tees
Brignall

Reeth

West Burton

River Swale
Muker

River Ure

River Nidd

Great Whernside

6

MarketPlace: **AUK**	Order Number: **204-0314516-1591573**
Order Date: **2016-04-27**	Email: **459trrfzdx36mxt@marketplace.amazon.co.uk**

Items : 1

Item		Locator
Witches in Old North Yorkshire [Paperback] [1987]	OD	HOL-3-LM-071-04-38
ISBN : 0907033547		

PrintID: 100002468843

Chapter 1

Eerie Doings in East Cleveland

One stormy night at the end of the 18th century, Farmer Oughtred and his household were sitting snugly in the farm kitchen at Hob Hill, a couple of miles outside the village of Marske. Rushlights dipped and quivered in the draught, casting odd-looking shadows. Not a night to be out of doors.

Suddenly, there came a thunderous knocking at the front door of the farmhouse.

'Answer it, lass!' Farmer Oughtred jerked his head in the direction of their little maidservant. Obediently, the girl rose from her sewing and went into the hall. They heard her pull back the heavy bolts and open the door. 'A wild night for callers,' thought the farmer to himself. 'Strangers, too. A neighbour would have come to the back door.'

There was a scream. The little maid came running into the kitchen, her eyes wide with terror. An icy blast from the open door swirled around the kitchen.

'Maister, maister, 'tis a demon, a demon at the door!' Oughtred was on his feet. 'Hast shut t' door?' he demanded. The child was too frightened to speak but she shook her head. The farmer, angry and more than a little nervous, went to the door himself, looked outside, shut and bolted the door. He came back into the kitchen.

'There's nought outside,' he said. 'What didst see, lass?' The maid was sobbing now. ''Twas like a pig, but all a-fire,' she stammered. ''Twas like a picture of the bad place, 'twas a demon from the bad place!' Then followed a crash from the parlour. This time there was something to be seen when they went in. Mrs. Oughtred's best china tea-service was in pieces on the floor.

'Evil's come into this house,' declared Oughtred. 'We've not seen the last of it.' He was right. This was only the beginning of many breakages in the Oughtred household. The farm suffered too. Their winnowing machine needed the blacksmith's hand, horses went lame, cattle sickened, milk yield went down.

Oughtred and his family had no doubt whatever about who had caused this havoc. It was the local witch, Peggy Flounders. Witches were known to be in league with the Devil. Peggy must have sent that demon to their farmhouse, in revenge for something they'd done to displease her.

Peggy lived alone in a little cottage at the top end of Marske High Street. She was a weird-looking creature with a mass of hair on her chin, like a man. Older villagers could remember her coming to the village as a young woman, remember her three children, all 'base-begotten' (born out of wedlock). The eldest, George Davison, was still in the village though he'd taken to a respectable trade as a shoemaker. When Henry Flounders, a market gardener, had taken her on as his second wife, everyone had hoped she'd settle down and become a respectable wife and mother.

Henry, unfortunately, had disappeared. Whether the press-gang had got him (they were very active on the north-east coast at the end of the 18th century) or whether he'd taken to the sea to be out of the way of Peggy's notoriously bad temper, no-one was quite sure. Left on her own, Peggy's temper hadn't improved and she had the reputation of being able to make all sorts of nasty things happen to those she disliked.

What was Farmer Oughtred going to do about it? There was no question of calling in the Law. In previous centuries, there had been laws against the practice of witchcraft, though there were remarkably few prosecutions in North Yorkshire, far fewer than in the rest of England. Now, after 1736, witchcraft was no longer a punishable offence. The Law no longer believed in the power of witches but the majority of people living in country districts had different ideas. Witchcraft, to them, was a real menace. They needed a remedy.

Farmer Oughtred's remedy was only a mile away, at Upleatham. Jonathan Westcott (or Westwick as he appears in local records) was a gamekeeper but he ran a side-line, practising as a Wise Man. There were quite a number of these Wise Men in North Yorkshire during the 18th and early 19th centuries. They dealt in the supernatural but used it for good, not evil, purposes. They offered magical cures for a variety of ailments, offered to trace missing articles, particularly those stolen, and to trace missing persons. They cast horoscopes, predicted the future and most important they offered to deal with any problem caused by witchcraft.

So Farmer Oughtred made his way to Upleatham and called on Jonathan. The sight of Master Westcott, dressed in his magician's robes, surrounded by his impressive-looking equipment, would be reassuring to his witch-ridden client. Jonathan listened to the tale of woe and agreed that Peggy was responsible. He would come and perform some counter-magic to neutralise the evil spell. Would Farmer Oughtred provide a black fowl?

Jonathan arrived at Hob Hill farm. He ordered that every door and window be closed and tightly sealed. Then he got to work on the black cock. It was pierced with nine new pins, then placed on the fire in the farm kitchen. It had to be reduced to a cinder, exactly at midnight, which must have taken a bit of careful timing but Jonathan was an expert at such things. Some kind of incantation went along with the burning of the fowl, but Jonathan, like most Wise Men, discouraged his clients from talking about exactly what happened during the ceremony, explaining that the counter-magic wouldn't work if details were made public.

After Jonathan's visit, all was well in the Oughtred household, but the Upleatham Wise Man had other clients from Marske. Hannah Rothwell and Mary Parker were neighbours of Peggy Flounders. They too had trouble.

Both had fallen out with the old witch and nobody in the village was surprised when Mary's cow went dry and Hannah's butter wouldn't 'come' though she churned until her arm was tired. Jonathan agreed with them that Peggy was the culprit but this time his counter-magic was less spectacular. Jonathan was very good at making his remedies fit the needs of his clients.

Hannah was told to wash out her butter churn three times, once with boiling water, once with boiling water and salt, once with water and a handful of rowan berries. It was well known that salt had magical properties. The rowan tree (or mountain ash) was equally well known to protect people from being affected by a witch's spell. Farmers used to keep rowan wood in their cow byres. Jonathan told Hannah to cut little plugs of rowan and drive them into her churn at certain places.

When all was done, Hannah had to turn her churn nine times, as if she was making butter, reciting, as she did so, the following 'nominy' (jingle):

> 'This time it's thine,
> Next time it's mine,
> And mine for evermore.'

Jonathan's cure worked. Whether it was that Hannah's churn got an extra good clean out in the process or whether salt, rowan and incantation did the trick, is a matter of opinion. Hannah and her friends had no doubt about it.

Jonathan was a little less confident about his cure for Mary's cow. He advised that it should be given a good dose of opening medicine. Then it was to have gentle exercise. She should lead it up and down the grass-covered roadside where it grazed along with other Marske villagers' cows. She shouldn't milk it too energetically for nine days. On the tenth day, she was to milk it as usual but first, she must whisper in its ear,

'Ah's milking thee for Peggy Flounders.'

However, if this remedy failed, said Jonathan, the fault lay in the cow, not the witch and she must make the best of it, getting rid of the animal somehow.

Peggy was once known to have performed her own 'counter-magic,' rubbing out, as it were, her own spell when she felt more friendly towards its object. A certain Farmer Pearson vexed her and she 'wished a bad wish on him.' When

The church of St. Germaine, Marske-by-Sea, in the churchyard of which Peggy Flounders lies buried. The church was demolished in 1956, leaving only the tower standing. Photo by L. Anderson.

A section of the Zetland Estate survey map, 1815, showing the cottage occupied by Peggy Flounders, the Marske witch. The original document ZNK 3/1/27 is in the North Yorkshire Records Office, Northallerton. Reproduced by courtesy of the Marquis of Zetland.

his cattle started dying off, one by one, from no apparent cause, the village knew who was to blame. His losses put poor Farmer Pearson out of business and he handed over his farm to a cousin.

When the cousin arrived to take over, he was horrified to see Peggy waiting for him at the gate. This would put paid to his chances of success. However, Peggy had a smile for him.

'Thoo ez mah good wishes,' she told him graciously. Then she took off her long red cloak, jumped over it and muttered some words that nobody heard because nobody was reckless enough to go near enough. The new farmer had no problems and the village put it down to the fact that Peggy had kindly cancelled the spell laid on his farm.

All in all, Marske had little reason to be sorry when, in 1835, Peggy came to the end of her days, aged 85. They laid her in the churchyard of St. Germaine, overlooking the sea. Rev. Joseph Harrison, Marske's vicar, would know all about her reputation but it didn't prevent him from giving Christian burial to the old lady. Like the Law, the Church had ceased to take witchcraft seriously.

There were whispers of witchcraft in the little village of Kilton, many years ago. Even in the 20th century, stories have been told of a witch in Kilton woods, but those who tell such stories, heard from their parents and grandparents, feel that the Witch of Kilton woods is more like a ghost, perhaps conjured up by those who passed through the woods when they were 'market-merry' (that is, after they had celebrated a day at Guisborough market with a glass or two of ale).

There were plenty of witches in Guisborough at the time when Marske was suffering from Peggy Flounders. In those days, the chemist's shop was kept by a Quaker gentleman who found his customers rather superstitious in their views. It distressed him when, one morning, an elderly lady called at the shop and suddenly became very agitated when she dropped something out of her purse and couldn't find it on the shop floor.

'It's my bit of witch wood (rowan wood),' she explained. 'It will never do to be without my bit of witch wood,' and she went on her hands and knees searching for it.

'Why Mally,' protested the chemist gently, 'You surely don't believe in witches any more.'

'Not believe in witches!' declared the old dame indignantly, 'I tell you, there's eleven of them in this town at this moment.'

There was certainly a Witch Bridge near Whitby Lane, Guisborough, in old Mally's time. Records in 1781 tell of it being repaired though there are no stories about the witch who gave it that name. There was, however, a witch prosecuted at Helmsley in 1657 who had come from Guisborough (his story is told in chapter 6).

One of old Mally's witches was known as Jane Greer. In her youth she must have been a beauty, was well known as a neat dancer, could show a pretty ankle and was popular with the men folk. She was less popular in old age. A local poet wrote,

'She's ugly as muck wi' black blood in her heart,
Old Scrat (i.e. the Devil) bought her soul, so they say.'

11

Oddly enough, in spite of this reputation, the only piece of witchcraft recorded of Jane is her ability to turn herself into a hare, something that most North Yorkshire witches were credited with being able to do, Peggy Flounders included. Some of these witches did damage when they were scampering about the countryside in the shape of a hare but Jane doesn't even seem to have done that. In fact, she seems more to have given the local sportsmen a run for their money.

A tale is told of how a group of Guisborough men chased a hare from Scaling Dyke to Stanghow, a distance of 20 miles. When after strenuous efforts, by both men and dogs, the hare managed to get away from them, they were all convinced that it had been Jane Greer herself. How else could a mere hare have managed to escape such skilled hunters, such well-trained dogs? It must have been witchcraft, the only explanation for anything that went against natural laws.

They nearly got Jane once. She reached the door of her cottage, the dogs hard at her heels. How was she going to open it in her hare-shape? Nothing for it but to jump through the key-hole. A dog grabbed her just as she leapt. Poor Jane bore the scars of that encounter to the end of her life.

An extraordinary story, isn't it? Richard Blakeborough, to whom it was told in the late 19th century, found it a little hard to swallow. It must, he said, have been an exceptionally large key-hole, or Jane had managed to turn herself into an extremely small hare. Even more extraordinary is that it was told to Mr. Blakeborough as fact. Such was the fear of witches that no super-human feat was believed to be beyond their powers.

Chapter Two

Witchcraft around Whitby

Jane Greer's adventure as a hunted hare took her to Scaling Dyke. Let us, then, follow the Whitby Road and turn off at Ugthorpe, for it was there that Ann Allen lived in the 1770's. She was a newcomer to the village, so when things began to go wrong, suspicion naturally fell on her rather than on anyone born in the village whose reputation was well known.

Ann kept pigs. She was a woman in her thirties, unlike Peggy Flounders and Jane Greer whose witch activities occurred in old age. Before long, Ugthorpe cow-keepers noticed that their animals were giving less milk than usual. Cows were grazed on common land so it wasn't difficult for dishonest people to help themselves to milk from an animal not their own. Ann's pigs looked suspiciously well nourished. A watch was kept on her but no-one saw anything to connect Ann with the vanishing milk supplies.

What, then, was wrong with the Ugthorpe cows? Something uncanny must be happening and, unlike the people of Marske, the village cow-keepers decided to consult their local priest. He must have been rather an old-fashioned gentleman in his ideas, or perhaps, like Jonathan Westcott, he was aware that his flock firmly believed in the power of devils. He said that he thought a devil must have taken hold of the Ugthorpe cows by their tails. Prayer would help to ease the situation. If cow-keepers would contribute a small sum to Church funds he would say a Mass in honour of a certain saint. Then, without doubt, the Saint would send an angel to chase away that devil. This idea didn't appeal to the cow-keepers because it involved hard cash. Like all good Yorkshire folk, they were thrifty.

At last, one cow went completely dry and its owner decided to take matters into his own hands. He went to Ann's cottage and accused her of milking his cow. Ann swore she'd never been near the animal. Tempers rose. Finally, the angry man picked up Ann's milking stool and threw it at her.

A stream of milk poured out of one of its legs. There was a shout of triumph from the crowd of fellow sufferers who had followed him into Ann's cottage.

'She's a witch! That's how witches do it!'

They were convinced that Ann had been milking the cow by remote control. It was a common belief in those days, in Scandinavia as well as England. A witch had only to hold a milking stool in her hands, say the name of a certain cow and its milk would be magically transferred into the stool. (A log of wood or a length of rope was just as effective, in the hands of a witch).

No-one had any doubt about Ann's guilt. She couldn't be punished by law, of course, because laws against witchcraft no longer operated. They dealt with her themselves. The milking stool was confiscated and burnt, publicly, on the moor, just beyond the high end of the village. Ann was sentenced to walk three times up and down the village street wearing nothing but her shift (under-garment). Everyone turned out to watch.

That would be the end of the story, but for the Lythe Parish Register. That tells us of a marriage in 1779 between Ann Allen and Robert Atkinson, so Ann

13

must have had one friend in all that hostile crowd. They didn't have a very long married life, though. In 1786 a sad series of burials appear in the register. First Ann's son, Thomas, then Ann herself, then her baby daughter, all in the space of three months. Robert only survived them for three years.

The curious thing about this information is that it reveals that Robert was a carpenter. Carpenters made milking stools. Had there been anything unusual about Ann's milking stool that made it leak milk when hurled into the air? If there was, its secret died with the Atkinson family.

Some witches were believed to help themselves to milk with the aid of a 'familiar' such as a hare, or a hedgehog. These familiars were supernatural assistants, given to the witch by her master, the Devil, to help with the bad work. There was a witch in Eskdale who had such a creature.

One hare was doing a lot of damage to a plantation of trees in the dale. Farmers tried to shoot it but no ordinary shot-gun pellets seemed able to hit it. On the advice of a Wise Man, one farmer loaded his gun with shot made from fragments of a silver coat button. Silver shot was the only way to hit a supernatural creature, he said. (You could, perhaps, argue that lead was cheap ammunition, silver was precious and the marksman would take better aim so as not to waste the charge.)

The silver-shot did the trick. The hare was shot dead. At the moment that shot was fired, neighbours said that the witch, in her cottage, screamed out, 'They have killed my familiar spirit!' and fell dead on the floor.

That story is easier to account for than those that tell of witches turning themselves into hares. In these days, it is quite common to hear of lonely people who befriend and become very attached to wild creatures. It happened in the olden days as well. The 16th century poet John Skelton describes a pet sparrow, killed by a cat, which gave its owner great grief. Here was a lonely old woman and a pet hare that came to a sad end. Could not the shock have been too much for her?

Witches did not always suffer when their familiar spirits were attacked. At Ruswarp, some time between 1775 and the early 19th century, there lived a witch who was believed to have had a whole tribe of demon assistants. She was Old Kathy. Everyone in the village was terrified of her. It wasn't even safe to let her catch a glimpse of you. As for crossing her threshold, no villager would dare to set foot on it. When she took it into her head to walk on the moors, wise people kept well away.

There must, however, have been some bold soul who didn't follow the general rule. How else could the story have got around that explained why there was one person in the district who was not afraid of Old Kathy. This person was Abe Rogers, a pedlar. He wasn't a local man but he went round the villages selling pins, needles and any small items that housewives could be in need of.

One day, he met Old Kathy on the moor. No-one knows exactly how it happened but there was a fierce argument between them. Perhaps she wanted to buy but the price wasn't right. She drew a knife and tried to stab the pedlar. Abe wasn't a young man but he was well able to defend himself. He grabbed

Kathy, flung her to the ground and threatened to strangle her if she didn't let go of the knife.

Kathy screamed out some abracadabra or other. Then the two of them were surrounded by weird unearthly creatures. They closed in on Abe, encouraged by Kathy's yells, 'Don't let him get away!' Abe stood his ground. Out of his pack he took a pinch of something and hurled it into the air. Immediately there was a whirlwind. Little bits of a gritty sustance flew about and got into the eyes of Kathy and her body-guard. Abe made his escape but not before he'd done a bit of damage to those impertinent demons — cutting off an ear or two.

Ever after that, Abe called on Kathy whenever he was in Ruswarp, walked into her cottage as bold as you like. Naturally, no-one ever knew what passed between them. It doesn't seem to have encouraged the village to have less fear of their old witch. Rather strange because Abe had shown that his magic was just as effective as hers.

What did happen on the moor that day? Was it a fight between witch and wizard? There is a simpler explanation. One thing a pedlar would carry in his pack would be a supply of pepper — or was it snuff? Who were Kathy's demons? Unlike the Eskdale witch, Kathy herself seems not to have been injured when Abe used her knife on those 'familiars' of hers.

Ruswarp people remembered Old Kathy for years after her death. About a hundred years ago, someone made a model of her, to show future generations what she looked like. This doll formed part of the visual aids used by Whitby schoolmaster John Hall when he gave Local History lessons. It is now in Whitby Museum, the only likeness of a North Yorkshire witch that is known to represent a particular individual.

Whitby is an ancient town so it is fitting that her first recorded witch should have lived in Elizabeth I's time. What's more, she was a titled lady, wife of Sir Francis Cholmley who came to live in Whitby round about 1570 when he inherited his father's estate. She was born Jane Bulmer and was not very popular with the Cholmley family. Richard's father had disapproved so strongly of the marriage that he entailed his estate shortly afterwards.

Jane was certainly the dominant partner. Memoirs of Sir Hugh Cholmley record:

'Francis Cholmley was exceedingly overtopped and guided by his wife which it is thought she did by witchcraft or some extraordinary means.'

There was even a whisper that Sir Francis, who died in 1579, might have survived a little longer if it hadn't been for his witch-wife. Her ladyship died seven years after her husband and it is anybody's guess how she employed those years as a widow. At all events, there was no court case over her doings, even although witchcraft was then officially a crime.

In the early 19th century, there was another witch living in the Whitby area whose familiar was a huge black cat. Neighbours were just as afraid of this monstrous creature as they were of its mistress. There is a certain risk in having people terrified of you, as many a dictator has found to his cost. Fear can make folk submissive or it can make them desperate. That's when bullies are liable to be victims of an 'accident.'

This witch seems to have been well aware of the danger. She protected herself

A doll representing Old Kathy, witch of Ruswarp. The original can be seen in Whitby Museum. Photo by courtesy of Whitby Gazette and Whitby Literary and Philosophical Society.

in a rather cunning way. Her speciality was foretelling the future and she made it known that, on the night she died, there would come a great storm. She added that she did hope, when that storm came, all sailors would have a good ship under them and all landsmen a good roof over them. How wise of her. Storms were dreaded by all. No-one would want that prophecy to be fulfilled one day before it had to be. They might be afraid of the old witch, but they wished her a long life. The strange thing is that, on the night she did die, there was a violent storm. The north-east coast is noted for them, of course.

Belief in witchcraft lingered long in the Whitby area. There is an interesting story told by the late Shaw Jeffrey, in 1923. A friend of his, Dr. Thomas English (1865-1937), was consulted by one of his patients. He found the man feverish and diagnosed an attack of influenza. The patient was, however, quite sure that wasn't the trouble. He'd been to Whitby market a few days previously and seen a young woman who had turned the 'evil eye' on him. No ordinary medicine was going to undo the spell cast by that evil eye.

'Your father was good at remedies for the evil eye,' he told the doctor. 'Happen he taught you a bit about them.' Dr. English could see that the old man believed himself to be under a spell. Patients have to have confidence in remedies prescribed. So he replied, 'Yes, my father taught me some of the old remedies. I'll mix one for you and put it in a bottle as if it was an ordinary prescription. But mind you don't tell anyone about it. Those remedies never work if they're talked about.'

Dr. English went into his dispensary and mixed the usual remedy for influenza. He handed over the bottle and hoped for the best. His patient was soon recovered. This story is confirmed by Brenda English in her biography of the English family. She adds that Dr. Thomas English (her father) was rather amused at being asked to prescribe a 'Wise Man's' remedy. 'I'm not the seventh son of a seventh son,' he said. (Wise Men often used to claim that they were seventh sons and that was where they obtained their special powers). He was, perhaps, a wise man in quite another sense.

That incident happened less than a hundred years ago. There are in fact several stories that show Dr. English's patient was not alone in his belief that there were people with this sinister ability to cause illness simply by looking at their victim. In Robin Hood's Bay at the end of the 19th century there were said to have been two very powerful witches. Richard Blakeborough recorded stories about them and felt it would not be tactful to publish their real names, so recently had they been in operation.

One witch was a man, said to have a very powerful evil eye. Even his wife felt she needed protection against it and so, every morning, she used to go and lay her hand on a rowan tree in their garden. It kept her safe for the day. This husband of hers once had a row with a neighbour from whom he'd borrowed a horse. He had been ungrateful enough to make some critical remarks about the animal, which were, of course, repeated to the lender. Tempers ran high and the neighbour threw a poker at him. The poker was seen to shatter into three pieces in mid-air. Even more astonishing was the fact that when he took it to the blacksmith for repair, the blacksmith was quite unable to do the job. He

17

Mulgrave Woods, the legendary haunt of Jeannie the demon-witch. Photo reproduced by courtesy of Cleveland County Libraries from John Walker Ord's 'History of Cleveland' (1846).

complained that he felt a pain shoot up his arm, like an electric shock, when he laid the pieces on his anvil.

The other witch was a woman and she too had a quarrel with one of the villagers. She wanted to buy a couple of ducks, but their owner refused to sell them to her.

'Thoo'll never have another bid for them,' threatened the witch.

Sure enough, the following week there was a thunderstorm and both ducks were struck by lightning.

The saddest witch story in this area comes from Fylingthorpe, a very isolated village in the late 19th century with no railway nearer than six miles away. There was a man in the village who firmly believed that he had the Evil Eye and was frightened to look at anyone in case he did them any harm. So he went about with head bent and eyes fixed to the ground. It was said he was very fond of children but kept well out of their way in case he was tempted to look at their innocent young faces. He would never have forgiven himself if he'd had a friendly chat with a youngster and then learnt that the child had taken ill or fallen into the stream. It would be his fault and it mustn't happen.

What a deep-rooted belief he must have had in the power of the Evil Eye if he felt it was something over which he had no control whatsoever. This unfortunate man was a witch against his will, or so it seemed to him. We can smile or, if we are more generous, feel very sorry for such a person but aren't there still, in the 20th century, people who suffer from fears that the rest of us consider quite irrational?

All these witches were real people, whatever we may think of the powers that their neighbours believed them to have had. Many of their names appear in official records. Others were known personally by those who told of their doings. There are, however, others so far back in local history that they appear as characters in a half-forgotten story, a legend rather than a piece of history.

Such was Jeannie of Mulgrave. She lived in Mulgrave woods and it is said she was such a nuisance to the farmers round about that one young man volunteered to go into the woods and deal with her. He mounted his horse, rode to the cave where she lived and shouted to her to come out. Out she came, so fiercely that the lad lost all his courage, turned his horse and galloped for his life. Jeannie came after him, travelling as fast as he could go. He made for the stream because witches lose their power if you cross running water. As he reached the bank, she caught up with him, struck the horse a mighty blow with her staff. It cut the poor beast in half but the pieces held together until horse and rider were over the stream. Then it dropped dead on the other side.

This story reminds you a little of the one about Tam O'Shanter, in Robert Burns' great poem. Did the local story-teller get his inspiration from Burns or could it possibly be the other way round? Burns did use folklore material from English sources.

In the 18th century (1708 is the date given), there was a witch, or a Wise Woman, living at Hinderwell not far from where Jeannie is supposed to have lived. It is rather difficult to distinguish between witches and Wise Women sometimes. If you go by the general principle that witches used their powers for evil purposes whereas Wise Women always aimed at doing good, it still isn't easy to decide about this Hinderwell magic-worker.

One day, a certain Master Slamper called on her. He had had a quarrel with his girl friend and he wanted a spell cast on her that would spoil her beauty. 'Very well,' he was told, 'I shall see to it for you. Now go home.' Master Slamper set off home in high spirits. To reach home, he had to pass through Roxby churchyard.

That was where he came to grief. Waiting for him, amongst the tombstones, was a crowd of unearthly creatures. They seemed like ghosts, at first, but after they'd chased and caught him, he found they were a bit more solid than ghosts. They had broomsticks and gave him such a good thrashing that he carried the marks of it on his skin for the rest of his life. Had that spiteful Master Slamper consulted a witch or a Wise Woman? It's a matter of opinion, isn't it?

Staithes had a very practical way of dealing with their local witches. If a coble or fishing smack had had a run of bad luck, the fishermen took it for granted that a local witch was responsible. The owners of the unlucky boats gathered together at midnight, killed a pigeon, took out its heart, stuck the heart full of pins and burned it over a charcoal fire.

When the pigeon's heart had been reduced to ashes, they all waited to see who would come to the door. Whoever it was, would be the witch who had ill-wished their boats. She would have been drawn to the house by the power of the spell they had cast.

When she arrived, they didn't set about her as the 'ghosts' set about Master Slamper. That would have been counter-productive. They gave her a small

The churchyard at Hinderwell, where Master Slamper came to grief. Photo reproduced by courtesy of Cleveland County Libraries from J. A. Atkinson's 'History of Cleveland' (1874).

Nineteenth century Staithes, where they had a way with witches. Photo reproduced by courtesy of Cleveland County Libraries from J. C. Atkinson's 'History of Cleveland' (1874).

present, to gain her good will. Then, when the boats had better luck, it showed that the witch had appreciated their gift. Not many Yorkshire countrymen tackled their witches in such a humane way.

In the days of sailing boats, Yorkshire fishermen are said to have 'bought' winds from witches. These took the form of a piece of string with knots in it. When you needed a wind, you undid a knot and there it was.

Staithes fisherfolk used to call upon Wise Men sometimes when they had had something stolen. In 1882, the bell man at Staithes was asked to give out the following notice:

'Stolen yesterday afternoon a large fisherman's net belonging to Jack. If it is not brought back by tomorrow at 1 p.m. he'll apply to the Wise Man at Scarborough.'

This was, of course, after Jonathan Westcott's time (Upleatham would have been a lot nearer to go for assistance). However, it was most unlikely that Jack would have to carry out his threat. Such was the reputation of those Wise Men that the thief would see that Jack's net was back where it belonged before the dead-line ran out.

Chapter Three

Sorcerers round Scarborough, Ryedale and Goathland

There are records of witches in the Scarborough area as far back as the days of Charles I, when laws against witchcraft, introduced in James I's reign, were very harsh indeed. All dealers in magic were condemned as having sold themselves to the Devil. Even if spell casting was done to help people, rather than injure them, those who indulged in sorcery could be prosecuted. Indeed, Authority felt that 'white' witches should be dealt with more severely than those who worked evil with their spells. Evil-working witches were, naturally, feared and shunned by all decent people but many ordinary folk might be tempted to consult a white witch if their problem couldn't be solved by ordinary means.

This is what happened in the little village of West Ayton, five miles south-west of Scarborough in the year 1634. A woman called Barbara had lost some articles of clothing and was convinced they had been stolen. It wasn't easy to get help in such cases in those days, there being no such thing as the C.I.D. However, something could usually be done about getting stolen property back, once you knew who'd taken it and where it was being hidden.

So Barbara consulted some friends of hers — Jane Kitchen, Mary White, Barbara Deighton and Anne Maddison, all ordinary housewives like herself, but they'd had some experience in the casting of spells. The ladies agreed to help. Unfortunately Authority got to hear about their activities, all four were arrested and had to appear at Thirsk Quarter Sessions, to answer the charge of: 'taking it upon themselves to tell one, Barbara Temple, by witchcraft, charms or sorceries, where and by whom stolen and taken from her certain clothes were to be found.'

There is no record of a punishment having been imposed. Perhaps the Thirsk Justices simply warned the four witches not to attempt such a thing again — it was against the law. We don't know exactly how the ladies set about their task as witch-detectives but you will hear about how the Sowerby Wise Man went about it, a couple of centuries later, in Chapter 6.

A much more serious accusation of witchcraft happened at Scarborough, in 1652, which resulted in a full-scale witch trial. It happened on the day of Scarborough Fair. John and Ann Allen, of Scarborough, went to the fair, taking with them their four-year-old daughter. The little lass was tired before it was time to come home and John carried the child home on his shoulders. What a good view she would have of all that was going on! One sight alarmed her, though. A woman gave her a 'funny look.'

Not long afterwards, the poor little mite began to take violent fits. Witchcraft was suspected. Mrs. Allen was advised to seek help from one Elizabeth Hodgson, who professed to be able to help in cases of the Evil Eye. There was no doubt that the child was seriously ill. Mrs. Allen got a young serving maid to sit up with the child all one night. The maid reported that she had counted 40 attacks of shivering and spasms, after each of which the little girl had seemed frightened and tense.

Elizabeth Hodgson declared that the child was bewitched. She even named the witch responsible — a woman called Ann Marchant, alias Hunnam. Ann Marchant was arrested and was searched for witch-marks. It was widely believed that those who had sold themselves to the Devil always carried special marks on them, in the form of teats through which they suckled their familiar spirits.

Ann Marchant was found to have 'a blue spot which grew out of her flesh at her waist of great bigness.' Things looked very black for Ann. In some parts of England, that would have been accepted as positive proof that she was a witch, and she would most probably have been hanged. Not many years before this case, the notorious witch-finder Matthew Hopkins had been responsible for the execution of over 200 women on whom he had found similar marks. Fortunately, Master Hopkins had never crossed the border into Yorkshire, and Justices of the North Riding were far from accepting such evidence in a witchcraft case.

Ann was put on trial. The account of her trial is a very strange one.

For one thing, Elizabeth Hodgson, who identified the accused woman as the person responsible for the child's illness, was not in court. Evidence of identification was given at second hand by Mrs. Allen. She told the court that Elizabeth had undertaken to lift the spell but on discovering that Mrs. Allen had told people about the offer, hastily cancelled it on the grounds that the counter-spell would now not work. (You may remember in Chapter 2 that Dr. English was aware of this belief that counter-spells must be cast in secret).

Of course, Elizabeth herself was breaking the law by offering to cast a counter-spell so it is not really surprising that she kept out of the way during the trial. There was plenty of evidence to show that Ann Allen's daughter was really ill but the justices were not satisfied that her condition had been brought about by Ann Marchant, in spite of the witch-marks found on her. Ann's defence was simple — she denied that she had intended or done any harm to the child. There is no record of what happened to Ann after the trial. She was fortunate that her case was heard by North Yorkshire justices.

One 19th century Scarborough witch had a curious history. Jane Nicholson was the daughter of a woman deeply influenced by Joanna Southcott, the eccentric leader of a religious sect who lived from 1750 to 1814. Joanna died after believing herself about to become the mother of a new Messiah. Jane's mother believed her own unborn child to be destined for great things — a Prince, no less. It must have been a terrible shock for her when baby Jane arrived. One can imagine what effect the mother's disappointment may have had on that most unwelcome girl child.

Jane had an extremely sinister reputation when she grew up. Scarborough fishermen who were unlucky enough to meet Jane on their way to their boats invariably turned back and did no fishing that day. Jane would be sure to have ill-wished them and their boats.

The district round Pickering had witches in plenty. We have a record of their names and deeds from a George Calvert who catalogued them in 1823. George

Emma Todd's crystal ball, which can be seen in the Ryedale Folk Museum, Hutton-le-Hole. Photo by T. Middlemass, courtesy of the Crosland Foundation.

Calvert really believed in their powers, although he admitted that some of his contemporaries 'doubted and scorned' the notion.

The most versatile of them was Mary Nares of Pickering. She is reputed to have been able to turn herself into a cat, she kept a familiar spirit, all the Black Arts were at her finger-tips, she possessed the Evil Eye and, a slightly more popular gift from the point of view of Pickering residents, she had a crystal ball which she used to foretell the future. The Parish Register of Pickering shows a Mary Nares in 1814 who, with her husband James, presented a baby daughter for baptism at the Parish church, but there is no positive evidence that this was indeed Pickering's witch.

It wasn't safe to let Hester Mudd of Rosedale get too close to you. She too had the Evil Eye. Dina Suggett of Levisham kept a familiar spirit, Sally Craggs of Allerton was another crystal ball expert and Emma Todd of Ebberstone was nearly as bad as Mary Nares. Anything that could be done by the Black Arts, Emma was prepared to do. Her crystal ball is in Ryedale Folk Museum.

Nan Scaife, of Spaughton Moor, near Hutton-le-Hole, had a grisly recipe for making magic cubes, used in fortune-telling. It was a lengthy process. She used ground bone from the skull of a hanged man and the blood of a bat, a bullock, a wild dove, a mole and an adder. The mixture had to be set aside for seven years, after the addition of a few more ingredients, such as a crab's eyes and a toad's heart. Then she cut it into slabs and carved magic signs on it. The slabs were thrown, like dice, and predictions made according to which way they fell.

Fortune-telling would not, perhaps, have made these ladies particularly unpopular but they had another more sinister practice. They would take orders for the making of little models of your rival (in love or business, it didn't matter which). The models were made out of pitch, bees-wax and bullock's blood. Then, you took a pin and decided what damage you'd like to do. Stick the pin in the model's head — your victim developed migraine, a pin in the foot and he went lame, and so on.

Sabina Moss, of Cropton, was another witch who used a crystal ball but George Calvert records a much more interesting story about her, than is suggested by such a commonplace piece of witch-equipment. The village firmly believed that Sabina had regular contact with Old Scrat (the Devil). One day, during an argument with His Satanic Majesty, Sabina was clever enough to get the better of him. Her triumph was short-lived. Old Scrat promptly pushed her into 'a great slop of mig' (i.e. a pool of liquid from a manure heap). Sabina, of course, came out of it giving off an entirely unattractive 'perfume.' After that, she became known as 'Mother Migg.'

Peggy Deuell of Hutton-le-Hole used to tell fortunes at Malton with another witch, called Old Susan. One day, a gentleman called Dowler thought he ought to try to turn Peggy from her evil ways. He lectured her at some length saying, 'These fortunes you pretend to tell are nothing but lies, aren't they?' Peggy promptly reminded Mr. Dowler of an incident in his early youth when he'd done something he was heartily ashamed of and had hoped the affair well buried in the past. After that, he gave up all attempts at reforming Peggy, who continued her fortune-telling with her dice, spin-wheel and magic book (there's a copy of it in Ryedale Folk Museum).

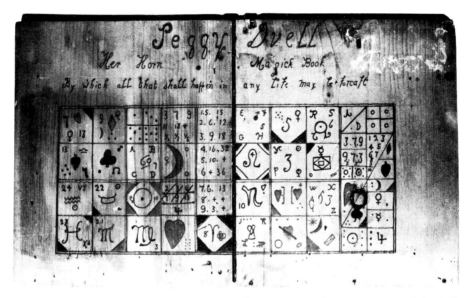

A nineteenth century copy of Peggy Deuell's 'magic book' from the Ryedale Folk Museum. Photo by T. Middlemass, courtesy of the Crosland Foundation.

Witchcraft in Ryedale is remembered even in the 20th century. An elderly gentleman in the 1960's recalled a witch called Nanny Pierson who was sometimes seen on the road to Hartoff. She had an irritating habit of bringing farm carts to an abrupt halt, by casting a spell on the horses, who came to a halt and refused to move until she lifted the spell. This appears to have been a common practice with witches if they had fallen out with the farmer. There was, however, a certain cure for it. Carters used to carry a whip made of rowan-wood. Touch the horse with a 'rowan-wood gad' and the witch's spell lost its power.

Goathland is famous for its witches. So energetic were they in the 18th and 19th centuries that the villagers felt they needed all the protective devices they could provide for themselves. In 1897, said F. W. Dowson, Goathland's historian, there was a farmer at Wheathill who kept 13 witch-crosses in his cow byre. They did him no good though — he went bankrupt. Mr. Dowson, writing in 1947, also told of a man who kept a bullock's heart stuffed with pins in the chimney of his house. He died in 1926. Some years after his death there was a slight difference of opinion between local historians about that bullock's heart.

Mr. Dowson described this man as 'the last believer in the Black Arts' (though he added that there were still villagers in the 1940's who weren't entirely sure that witchcraft was a thing of the past). Some people held this to mean that the bullock's heart was used to cast nasty spells on folk. However, W. Stonehouse, writing in 1880, mentions that it had, in former days, been a common belief that if you burnt a beast's heart stuck full of pins at midnight, it would draw witches from their hiding places, so perhaps the 20th century believer in witchcraft kept it on hand, like you might do a fire extinguisher, to use in case of need.

Goathland's witch was known as Nanny Pierson. There were, in fact, two witches of that name in the village, thought to have been mother and daughter. It is not, perhaps, surprising that the Rosedale witch was also known as Nanny Pierson because the surname was a very common one in Ryedale as well as Goathland, and many witches were known as 'Nanny,' a nickname for ladies who have reached grand-mother status.

It is difficult to identify either of the Pierson witches in the Parish Registers. There was an Ann Pierson, baptised in 1780, daughter of one John Pierson, a papist. This may well be Nanny the elder, because Richard Blakeborough gave it as his opinion that she was a member of the Church of Rome in her youth. If so she may be identified as the old lady called Ann Pierson who appears in the burial register in 1849.

Of the younger Nanny Pierson there is no sign. F. W. Dowson says, however, that she was remembered quite clearly by senior citizens of Goathland who died in the 1940's. It was, however, Nanny the elder who was the really vicious witch. It was said that she could cripple an unborn child. Of course, as medical science has learnt, a German Measles microbe can do that, so perhaps Nanny got the blame unjustifiably.

She did, however, try some very nasty tricks. The local squire had a daughter who fell in love with a young farmer. Squire didn't want the lad as his son-in-law. His daughter must make a rich marriage with an ugly old fellow. The girl, naturally, refused to see the thing her father's way. So Squire went to see Nanny Pierson.

As a result of his visit, or so the village thought, the girl was stricken with paralysis in her lower limbs, which prevented her from eloping with her boyfriend. The lad went to see the Scarborough Wise Man and received advice on how to cancel Nanny's spell. He was to get a drop or two of her blood, mix it with a few drops of holy water and apply the mixture to his lady's feet.

This made sense to the lad. It was believed that if you could draw blood from a witch, she lost her power over you. But how could he possibly get near enough to the old hag? This was, of course, in the early 19th century when witchcraft was no longer a punishable offence. Drawing blood from a fellow villager certainly would be frowned upon by the law. Then he had a bright idea. Nanny was known to be able to turn herself into a hare, like most witches. The lad lay in wait for her with the appropriate silver bullet, hit her and used the blood left on the grass as she scampered off.

He made his mixture, borrowed a ladder, climbed in through his true love's window (after making sure that Squire was out of the way) and anointed her feet. The spell was broken, and the lady recovered the use of her limbs. Richard Blakeborough commented, 'This, I believe, is the first recorded case of massage.'

Nanny Pierson bewitched another unfortunate young lady. This time it has been possible to identify her as the daughter of Gawain Pierson, yeoman farmer of Thornhill farm. Gawain had two daughters who survived childhood, Ann and Mary. The victim of Nanny's spite was probably Ann (perhaps Nanny didn't like the child having been given *her* name).

Ann had been confined to bed for three years. No-one knew exactly what ailed her except that it was Nanny's doing. Gawain persuaded his friend the schoolmaster to seek help from the Wise Man of Stokesley (more about him in chapter 5). The schoolmaster was decidedly sceptical. However, he got on his horse and made the journey, mainly to satisfy his friend. He arrived at the Wise Man's door and was somewhat shaken to be greeted with, 'Well now, tha's come ti see me about Pierson's lass who's dowly (i.e. ill).'

How could the Wise Man have possibly known that? He hadn't written to make an appointment. He was very frank with the Wise Man, said his friend believed the girl was bewitched but he himself didn't believe in witchcraft. 'Then tha'd better have stayed at home and mended thi' window,' replied the Wise Man. This really shook the schoolmaster. Before setting off, he'd had to chase a stray dog out of his house and a window had been broken in the process. He'd had the same thought as he set off — better stay at home and mend the window for all the good you're going to do — but he hadn't told anyone, not even his wife.

So impressed was the schoolmaster by this evidence of the Wise Man's powers that he carried out all the instructions given. He remained at the Wise Man's house all night. His host read some strange-sounding words from a large book. They sat in silence. Presently came a tapping at the window. The curtain was drawn back, an old hag's face was seen glaring into the room. With a gasp of amazement the schoolmaster recognised — the Goathland witch.

'I can clip her claws,' said the Wise Man. 'But you must swear never to reveal what you see or hear from now until morning.' The schoolmaster swore and kept his oath, so we don't know exactly how Nanny's claws were clipped.

The schoolmaster returned to Goathland and, sure enough, his friend's daughter was sitting up in bed, on the mend.

Another story about Nanny makes you feel a little sorry for the old horror. She was in the habit of going to Farmer Webster's kitchen every day for milk. Mrs. Webster had a goose, sitting on a clutch of eggs by the kitchen. When the goose saw Nanny, it bolted in terror, cracking one of the eggs. This happened every time Nanny appeared for her jug of milk. In the end, Mrs. Webster got advice. 'Put a drop of holy water in the jug along with the milk.' When she did that, an astonishing thing happened. The goose, instead of bolting, spread its wings and went for Nanny, who dropped the jug and was out of the door in a flash. They never had any trouble after that.

Nanny Pierson junior was a very different character. She was more a fortune-teller than a caster of spells, though people were still rather scared of her uncanny powers as a prophet and the weird tricks she could play. She was much in demand at 'card laaking do's' (card-playing parties). On one occasion, to please a little girl, she contrived to make herself so small that she could creep into the china cabinet at Church Farm House, and creep out again without breaking a single pot. You can imagine that Nanny junior would have made an excellent member of the Magicians' Circle of our own time. They are expert at such tricks, though they have far more sophisticated 'props' than Nanny could have had.

Another story tells of how Nanny rescued some sheep in a snow storm so severe that the shepherd hadn't dared go out in search of them. There must surely have been witchcraft in that episode. How else could a mere female have accomplished something that defeated an experienced shepherd?

The rocking-chair that belonged to Nannie Pierson junior of Goathland, now displayed in the Marske Folk Museum. Photo by Denise Robson, courtesy of J. Anderson.

Chapter Four

Nan Hardwick and other Eskdale Witches

In the days when witchcraft was a punishable offence, Justices in North Yorkshire were, as we have seen, inclined to be lenient with offenders. However there were places where the local inhabitants believed in sterner measures. Such a place was Danby in the 17th century. An old diary, quoted by Shaw Jeffrey, gives the following:

'5th October 1663. Molly Millburn was this day whipped for that she, being a witch, did work great evil amongst Thomas Turner's cattle so that a grievous scab broke out amongst them.'

Shaw Jeffrey had also some information about the less destructive activities of this Molly Millburn. She embroidered amulets, said to be able to protect the wearer from misfortune, could ward off evil spells cast by other witches and worked some remarkable cures on sick people.

Could this be the same woman? Danby parish registers have a record of only one Molly Millburn and she was a poor vagrant woman who died in 1616, following the birth of her illegitimate son. It could, of course, have been a descendant of hers.

Another diary entry, over a century later (so it cannot have been the same diarist), records another Danby woman receiving similar punishment. '27th Nov. 1797. George Langstaff soundly whipped Elsie Barker for causing an evil among his sheep. 4 died before he whipped her.'

One gathers that after George put his whip aside, no more sheep died. It must be admitted though, that the word 'witch' is not used in the case of Elsie Barker. In 1797 there was, legally, no such person as a witch though many country people disagreed.

Nan Hardwick was the most famous witch in Danby and is well recorded by Canon J. C. Atkinson, Danby's vicar from 1847 to 1898, who got his information from senior parishioners who remembered her. She lived at Spittlehouses, an isolated settlement in Danby Dale.

She cannot be identified with certainty in the parish register of Danby but it's likely that she was the daughter of Matthew Hardwick, baptised 12th May 1765.

In some of the stories about Nan, she certainly seems to have been more sinned against than sinning. The young bloods of the village were said to have entertained themselves by chasing her, as if she was an animal. She used to lie hidden in a clump of bushes near Ainthorpe. The lads then flushed her out and chased her down to the stream where it was apparently agreed to let the chase end.

One night, Thomas Prudom, a farmer's son, arrived too late to join in the game of Nan-chasing. So he stood across the path as Nan ran towards him, blocking the way with legs astride — just to see what she would do. The result staggered him in more ways than one. He heard her clogs on the stone path but couldn't see her. Then something rushed between his legs, knocking him over. He heard a satisfied chuckle from somewhere but Nan was nowhere to be seen.

Thomas's father wasn't any kinder to the old witch. Thomas Prudom senior was one of the overseers who allocated Parish Relief to needy cases. When Nan applied for Parish Relief he didn't consider her a needy case, and turned down her application. Some time after this incident, when he was walking home from Castleton he met Nan, just as he was crossing the stream that drains Danby Dale. The little bridge was then a primitive affair — no room for two people to pass. Prudom didn't see why a prosperous farmer like himself should give way to an old good-for-nothing like Nan. Although Nan had already reached the bridge, he stepped onto it — expecting her to step back.   Canon Atkinson describes what happened:

'Then her power fell on him and he stood like a statue, unable to move hand or foot until she was pleased to release him, which was not at once.' Witches are supposed to lose their power when you cross running water. Nan Hardwick must have been an exceptionally powerful witch, don't you think?

Another story shows Nan in a less attractive light. She went begging at a farm near Westerdale. They gave her bread and beer which she accepted with a 'thank-you.' The farmer's wife was, at this time, about to have her first baby. Nan put her head round the bedroom door.

'Thoo'll have a lad afore morning,' she told the farmer's wife. 'Thoo'll call him Tommy, won't tha?'

The farmer's wife said no, if the baby was a boy they'd planned to call him John.

'Ah, but tha'd best call him Tommy. Good day to you,' said the old witch and went on her way.

Later that day it was time to get the midwife, a sister of the woman in labour. The farmer harnessed his horse and gig and set off on the five-mile journey. He'd gone little more than half-way when the horse stopped at a bridge and refused to move. He tried to get down and lead the animal but found he too couldn't move a muscle.

Suspecting witchcraft the farmer called out, 'Nan, this is your doing. What art after?'

He heard Nan chuckle. 'You'll call the bairn Tommy or you'll not move a step further.'

The unfortunate man was in a quandary. If he didn't fetch his sister-in-law, his wife might well die in labour. On the other hand, it was a very firmly held belief that you must never change the name of a child once you'd settled on it. In the end, he agreed. If the child was a boy, his name must be Tommy. Immediately, the horse moved on and he was able to continue his journey.

That's where the story ends, unfortunately. Perhaps the couple solved their difficulty by having baby christened John Thomas — plenty of boy babies were called that. It is extraordinary though that Nan should have played such a cruel and pointless trick on a young couple that had done her no harm. Was it simply a desire to show off the strange power she had or did she believe that by forcing the couple to adopt her choice of name, it would give her power over the child in the future?

Nan played another spiteful trick at Lowna Bridge (a settlement between Hutton-le-Hole and Gillimoor). Nan had relatives there and one day she walked the 20 miles from Spittlehouses to visit them, arriving on the day when the daughter of the house was getting married. The house was full of guests and there was nowhere for Nan to sleep. A good-natured bridesmaid offered to let Nan share her bed.

The bride, hearing of her offer, was tactless enough to remark that *she* wouldn't fancy that old hag snoring beside her. Of course, Nan heard her. She snapped out, 'You'd not sleep with me — you'll not sleep with your bridegroom.' Sure enough, during the usual skylarking amongst the young folk that follows weddings, the bridegroom fell off a ladder and broke his leg. There is no evidence that Nan was directly responsible for this mishap but of course the whole family was convinced it was her doing.

Betty Strother was another witch who lived at about the same time as Nan Hardwick but there is some doubt as to where she lived. George Calvert records her as belonging to either Castleton or Blakey Ridge. The latter seems more likely since Canon Atkinson doesn't mention her at all in his account of witches who lived in his own parish of Danby. Betty was a 'white' witch of very good reputation indeed. She cured illnesses and dealt with demons. She is said to have firmly refused to supply the local 'Don Juan' with a love potion which he intended giving to a young girl he had his eye on.

Old Mally of Commondale was less popular. Like Ann Allen of Ugthorpe, she was believed to help herself to milk from other people's cows, but she did it in the shape of a hare. Neighbours had noticed an extra-large hare that entered the field where cows were grazing, hopping amongst them, quite at home. The owner of the cows, who had been getting worried at their low milk yield, loaded his shot-gun with the approved silver pellets (made out of a couple of silver buttons) and hid himself near the gap in the hedge where the hare had been seen to enter.

The hare duly appeared but instead of going towards the cows, it lolloped across to where the farmer was hiding. Its body seemed to get bigger, its eyes more fierce, with every lollop it took. This was no hare — it was a monster. The farmer panicked, threw aside his gun, fled home and locked the door. Old Mally seems as if she had a brand of magic not so different from Nan Hardwick on the bridge at Danby.

A witch-hare at Glaisdale Head was a vandal. It damaged young trees in a plantation, as hares will, but the damaged trees weren't chewed but cut, as if by a pen-knife, and left lying about. The owner went after that vandal hare with a shotgun. He fired, there was a brisk shriek and this time it was the hare that fled. Next day a certain Old Maggie was found to be ill in bed. She said she'd fallen on a broken bottle. Serve her right.

Nanny of Westerdale was an oddity because not only did she appear to be able to turn herself into a hare, she actually didn't object if the local sportsmen had a try at catching her. She met a group of them with their dogs and offered to tell them where they'd find a hare which would give them a grand run — but they mustn't on any account let slip a black dog at it. The lads found a hare, just where Nanny said it would be and it did indeed give them a splendid chase, though of course they didn't catch it.

Just as they felt they'd had enough for one day, a black dog appeared out of nowhere and made straight for the hare as it was running in the direction of

Westerdale Bridge, where they hunted Old Nanny in the shape of a hare. Photo reproduced by courtesy of Cleveland County Libraries from J. C. Atkinson's 'History of Cleveland' (1874).

Kildale Church, c.1874. Nanny Howe was seen flying overhead by people alive when this drawing was made. Photo reproduced by courtesy of Cleveland County Libraries from J. C. Atkinson's 'History of Cleveland' (1874).

Nanny's cottage. The dog grabbed the hare by the leg for an instant before it disappeared into Nanny's garden. Rather alarmed at having accidentally gone against Nanny's instructions, they called at the cottage to apologise and found Nanny with a wound in her thigh. How do you account for that? The sportsmen had no doubt about it.

Howe Wood, near Kildale, had been linked with witchcraft for many a long year. Several 19th century writers have recorded stories about it though these are more in the nature of folk legends, like Jeannie of Mulgrave's story, not first hand accounts by old people who remembered encounters with witches.

One such story seems to support the theory that early witches belonged to a religious cult of pre-Christian origin, as the late Dr. Margaret Murray believed was the case, and present-day witchcraft practitioners tell us they also believe. A local rhyme, current in the 19th century, says:

> 'The Devil with his imps
> His pleasure in the Kildale woods
> Three summer days did take.'

Stephen Howe, a Kildale yeoman, was bold enough to say that if he caught the Devil on his land he'd give him a thrashing. Somehow the Devil heard about it for he arrived one day in a magnificent black coach, drawn by six black horses. Stephen fled but his wife, Nanny, stood up to the Devil, taking a swipe at him with her broom.

However, the Devil soon swept Nanny off her feet (with his tail, it's said), declared he'd won and he'd carry off either Stephen or Nanny, it didn't matter which. Nanny said she'd go and rode off with him in the coach.

Did this story have its origin in a real incident? Some religious cult could have been performing its rituals, a man in black as their leader. If they were pagan rituals, then to orthodox Christians they were inspired by the Devil. Nanny may have been one of the band and their leader came to collect her when their activities became too well known for it to be safe to use Howe Wood any more as a venue for their gatherings.

Another story gives a delightful picture of an argument amongst the witches. Nanny Howe is said to have fallen out with her Satanic Master and chased him for miles on her broomstick. She would have caught him, too, but one of his attendant imps was quick-witted enough to 'hitch' a ride on Nanny's broom thus slowing her down enough for Satan to get away.

These stories lingered almost into the 20th century. Richard Blakeborough writing in the 1890's says he spoke to old people at Great Ayton who were quite sure that, in their youth, they actually saw Nanny Howe riding on her broomstick over Howe Wood. A kind of 19th century U.F.O. perhaps. Stranger things have been reported, even in our own day.

Chapter Five

Bewitchings in Bilsdale

Ingleby Greenhow, on the edge of Bilsdale, also has a witch legend, current in the 18th century and still remembered at the end of the 19th century when Richard Blakeborough heard it from two sources — the Scorer family of Basedale and the Vicar of Lastingham.

This legend tells how the women of Ingleby Greenhow were in great distress. Several babies had vanished from their cradles, never to be seen again. The villagers called in a local Wise Man, old Robbie Eskletts, who promised to look into the matter for them. He did so, and reported to a select group of village elders. Yes, it was the work of local witches. Robbie had seen a great stone on the moor, not far from Ingleby, on which a fire was burning. Moving in circles amid the smoke of the fire, were ravens, owls, hag-worms (i.e. adders) and strange non-human creatures called Aufs (elves). Three witches crouched by the stone, one of whom was Black Meg, well known to the village. One of the witches held up a living baby and flung it into the fire. Out of the fire crawled a black cat.

This, said Robbie, meant that the missing babies had been transformed into cats and Black Meg had them. The villagers must steal the cats from her and hide them in the church where Meg daren't go, it being holy ground. Then Meg's power must be broken. This was a long drawn out business. They needed a noble knight who had never in his life caused maiden or wife to blush. He would then have the power to vanquish a dragon, summoned up by Meg from the Bad Place.

Such a knight was found, the dragon died, Meg's house went up in flames and when the villagers ran to the church they found not Meg's cats but the missing babies. This story was turned into a 'Mell Act,' that is a play performed at the Harvest or Mell Supper celebrations. Richard Blakeborough searched for a script of the play but was unable to find one.

This legend is an odd mixture of black witchcraft, unholy rites performed by a witch group and something that resembles the stories of King Arthur's knights. Perhaps those who handed the story down had added a local legend to those told by travelling minstrels, centuries ago.

Great Ayton's witch was called Nanny. Some believe she was Nanny Garbutt (a common surname in the village in the 18th century and to be found all over Bilsdale, even today). She lived in a tumbledown cottage in a far corner of the Low Green, near the mill. She made no secret of the fact that she was in league with the Devil and the whole district went in terror of her.

An eerie tale is told about her dealings with a Stokesley woman, Mary Langstaffe. One day, Mary went to Kildale in order to look after her cousin Martha Sokeld, who had fallen ill. On the way she met Nanny. Not wishing to speak to this notorious character, she turned aside and pretended to pick flowers instead of bidding her good day. Nanny didn't like being ignored. 'Ah'll pay thee out!' she screamed, banging her stick three times on the ground.

Nothing dreadful happened to Mary there and then. She happened to have a bunch of rowan berries pinned to her dress, which, of course, protected her. She reached Kildale, Martha was soon over her illness and Mary returned to Stokesley. However, only two days later, Martha appeared at Mary's house, looking very ill indeed. She told her cousin that she believed she was dying but was determined to visit her sister at Northallerton before she died. A neighbour had given her a lift to Stokesley and she planned to rest overnight at Mary's house before going on to Northallerton by the carrier's cart.

Anxious to help her cousin, of whom she was very fond, Mary agreed to do some errands in Stokesley while she rested.

'Don't hurry back,' Martha told her, 'I'll maybe get a bit of sleep on the settle (settee) while you're gone.'

Something about her cousin's condition made Mary uneasy so she did the errands as quickly as possible and hurried home. She entered the house on tip-toe in case Martha was asleep, but her cousin was not lying on the settle. Instead she appeared to be crouched over the fire, a saucepan in her hand. Mary heard her muttering:

> 'It boils, thoo'll drink,
> He'll speak, thoo'll think,
> It boils, thoo'll see,
> He'll speak, thoo'll dee (die).'

In a flash, Mary realised this was not her cousin but the old witch. She was working a spell — against Mary and her boyfriend, Tom. She rushed into the room, caught up her Bible and held it high, crying out:

'You must do your worst. I hold by this!'

Immediately the witch overturned the saucepan into the fire, screamed out, 'Ye've escaped me but I'll get you yet!' and vanished.

Martha's body was found three days later on the moor head. Local people had no doubt about what had happened. Nanny must have enticed poor Martha onto the moor, 'spelled the soul out of her,' replaced it with her own black spirit and it was this diabolical combination which had called at Mary's house that morning.

Could such a thing happen? If not, what did give rise to this strange story? Martha was, no doubt, a very sick woman. Perhaps she arrived at Stokesley in a confused state of mind, near to physical collapse. While Mary was on her errands, perhaps she recovered enough to wander off, trying to make her way home, reached the moor where she collapsed and died. Nanny may have seen her go and taken the opportunity of slipping into the empty house. Her spells might be expected to work more effectively if performed in the home of their intended victim.

Nanny may or may not have had any part in Martha's death but she certainly did not succeed in harming Mary, who lived to be 85, had many children and grandchildren, one of whom told this story to Richard Blakeborough.

Whatever Nanny's actual powers were, her intentions seem to have been as bad as any witch's could be. Johnny Simpson of Newton-under-Roseberry called on her one day. His girl friend, Mary, had jilted him and got herself engaged to a certain Tom Smith. Johnny didn't want her back but he was set on spoiling the happiness of his rival. Nanny was willing to cooperate and made helpful suggestions.

Should she strike one or both of the happy couple with blindness? What about disfiguring Tom with a hare lip? If Johnny liked, she could contrive that the couple parted at the church door, never to be re-united. To do him justice, Johnny hadn't been intending to go that far. He wanted Nanny to bring ill luck to the wedding. He went through all the unlucky things that people always hoped wouldn't happen at their weddings.

'Make Tom drop the ring and let it roll onto a tombstone,' he said. ''When Mary has eaten her piece of cake and Tom has to smash the plate for luck, can you see to it that the plate stays in one piece? Nanny, make them quarrel on their wedding night and I swear I'll be your friend for life.' Nanny wasn't impressed.

> 'I've listened to you, now listen to me,
> All thee wants can be done, but I ken
> You're nowt but a ragget (good-for-nothing) of that I am sure,
> And I don't reckon much to aught that you'll swear,
> What's to do shall be done by thisen.'

So Johnnie received instructions for a piece of 'do it yourself' magic. He'd go to Ayton Bridge, wave Nanny's broom three times in the air, go backwards into the churchyard, collect some graveyard mould then wash his hands in the old well and leave Nanny's broom tidily beside it.

Johnny had begun to wish he'd never meddled with Nanny but he carried out his instructions to the letter, except for the last two items. Then he felt he'd done enough. He didn't wash his hands and he threw the broomstick into the beck. That was foolish of him. Witches are, we are told, sensitive about their broomsticks. Even when a witch borrows a broomstick from an unsuspecting housewife it is said she takes an interest in that broom ever after and is liable to cast a spell on the housewife should she mistreat it.

Johnny set off home and was followed by a whole host of creatures — bats, owls, skeletons. Then he met three 'night hags' who screamed at him that he was in their power because he'd disobeyed Nanny. They grabbed him, whisked him up to the top of Roseberry and tied Nanny's broom between his legs.

> 'You shall be hunted,' croaked they, 'By us and our familiars,
> We've owlets trained,
> A clutch of bats,
> Flay-bogles (ghosts) without feet,
> We've goblin dogs,
> And great big frogs,
> They'll all hunt thee — to-neet!'

Johnny finally reached home more dead than alive. It put him off meddling with witches for the rest of his life. Nanny did at least do that for him. The full story of John's experiences was told in 'The Hunt of Yatton Brig,' a magnificent narrative poem by Richard Blakeborough, very well known in Cleveland at the beginning of this century. It is often quoted but the less familiar parts of it have been reproduced here.

Great Broughton was another witch-infested spot. Nanny Newgill operated

'The night-hags meet Johnny Simpson.'

'The hunt is up.'

Four of Richard Blakeborough's drawings reproduced by courtesy of Cleveland County Libraries from 'The Hunt of Yatton Brigg' (1899) in their possession.

'Hurled down from Roseberry.'

'Dawn at Yatton Brig.'

in the early 19th century, rather later than Nanny of Great Ayton. She had an original line in 'shape-shifting,' that is the ability to assume a non-human form, being in the habit of turning herself into a hedgehog and stealing the milk from cows. It was a common belief that hedgehogs could suck milk from a cow's udder while it lay down in its pasture.

She had other tricks. A Broughton woman, Martha Brittain, developed severe aches and pains for which she believed Nanny was responsible. Henry Wilson, a local Wise Man, was consulted. He sent Martha to Stokesley, told her to buy a new fire shovel, chalk Nanny's name on it, then use it to bake a special cake over the fire. This had to be done with the windows and doors closed, of course, but surprisingly enough, Mr. Wilson said it had to be done, not at midnight as was usual for such counter-spell weaving, but at four o'clock in the afternoon.

At that time Nanny was weeding in a field, a mile away, with a group of other women. Just as the cake was cooked, Nanny was taken with violent stomach ache and had to go home where she remained ill for several days. Martha, on the other hand, lost all her aches and pains in the same moment as Nanny was afflicted. That takes a bit of accounting for doesn't it! There must, however, have been a reason for the cake cooking to have taken place while Nanny was out working, not at home in bed. You can be sure the whole village knew what was going on in Martha's cottage. Could Nanny's pains be induced by a bad conscience, Martha's by a conviction that the old woman wished her ill and had now been punished. Pain can be psychologically rather than physically produced.

There was one occasion when Nanny's innocence was proved to everyone's satisfaction. The sufferer was a Broughton man and he, too, consulted Henry Wilson. Someone had cast the Evil Eye on him. He wasn't sure whether Nanny or a man at Nunthorpe was responsible. Henry didn't express an opinion, but advised the man to tackle both of them about the matter, accusing them openly. Nanny looked her accuser straight in the eye and swore she'd never ill-wished him. The Nunthorpe witch was less convincing in his denials. So Henry and his client made a wax model of Mr. X of Nunthorpe and stuck a pin in one of his eyes. Sure enough, Mr. X's eye became violently inflamed; in fact he lost the sight of it altogether. The Broughton man was cured, of course.

Henry Wilson told his client that it was lucky for him that he'd guessed right. If Mr. X had not been guilty, the magic would have taken effect on his accuser, who would have been in a worse state than before.

Hannah Waugh, another Broughton witch, was definitely on the side of law and order. It was she who identified the Anngrove Hall murderer and openly challenged him with the crime. Anngrove Hall (known in 1823 as the Old Manor House) was near the Stokesley to Ayton road.

The murder story is a matter of legend, not reported in official records but is believed to have happened in the mid-18th century. The Squire of Anngrove Hall had a daughter who fell in love with her father's coachman, Henry Edwards. When the Squire found out, he gave the young chap his notice. But before Henry was due to leave, the Squire sent him to Stokesley with a box of

The Stokesley section of the map of Yorkshire published in John Graves 'History of Cleveland' (1808). The map shows the location of Anngrove Hall where a witch story took place.

valuable jewellery and orders to deliver it to a gentleman catching the London coach. Henry never returned from his errand.

It was, of course, assumed that the lad had made off with the valuables. The Squire set off in pursuit, issued a list of the missing items and offered a reward for information leading to the arrest of the thief, but neither they nor Henry Edwards were found. Henry had a sister, Polly, a maid at the Grange, half a mile from Anngrove Hall. She refused to believe that her brother could have

41

stolen his master's goods. Something must have happened to him. One night she returned to the Grange after her evening out white and shaken with a dreadful story to tell.

Polly had seen her brother's ghost. The ghost had its head battered in. No doubt at all in Polly's mind, her brother had been murdered. Who had done it? Her fellow servants pointed out that, like as not, there'd be a gang of them and they'd quarrelled over the loot. Polly would have none of that. Her brother was an innocent victim. She went to see Hannah Waugh. Hannah told her to get hold of a horse-shoe, one of those worn by a horse which her brother had tended and that had pulled the Squire's carriage when he set out in pursuit of the thief.

Hannah took the horse-shoe to the blacksmith and between them they did certain things with it, 'injected' magic as it were. Polly was then told to hang it up in some conspicuous place at Anngrove Hall. If the murderer came near it, he would be forced to reveal his guilt. Polly managed to do this without attracting too much attention. Then one day, her employers gave a party to which the Squire came. As he passed the spot where the horse-shoe hung, he staggered and became suddenly ill. That was enough for Polly.

The stolen jewels, the search, had been a cover-up. Squire had disposed of an unwanted future son-in-law.

Polly was ordered to hold her tongue. Squire was an influential man. Then Hannah herself took action. She met the Squire in Stokesley market. In front of everyone she said:

> 'You'll have your day,
> But lambs will play
> And skip where Anngrove stands,
> No lime shall hod (hold)
> Its stones, no sod
> Shall wrap up the deed of thy hands.'

A courageous act on the part of Hannah and it had its effect. Public opinion was on her side. The law did not accuse the Squire, his fellow men did. No servant would work at the Hall. Eventually he was forced to leave the neighbourhood and the Hall fell into ruins. Then, long afterwards, the remains of the unfortunate coachman were found, buried under the foundations of a hay stack on the Squire's land. The skull had been beaten in.

Peg Humphreys, the best known of Bilsdale's witches, does appear in early records. She started her married life at Kirkby in Cleveland where, in 1796, John Humphreys married Margaret Walker. The Humphreys farmed at East Moor in the 1830's. Peg had, they say, an uncanny appearance with a reputation to match. A man who had two close encounters with her witch activities was the famous Bilsdale hunter, Bobby Dowson (1816-1902). It was when Bobby was a teenage lad that he was out with Isaac Johnson after a hare. Near the Humphrey farm, they lost it and found Peg, very much out of breath.

She was very hospitable, asked them in and offered glasses of ale. 'I wouldn't hurt thee. Thoo's someone's bairn,' she reassured young Bobby. She doesn't seem to have taken to Isaac though. Shortly after the encounter, Isaac fell ill and died. Doctors weren't sure what had ailed him, but Bilsdale put it down to

Peg Humphreys. Were the lads really chasing Peg herself, like Danby youths had chased Nan Hardwick? Or did they really believe Peg had turned herself into the hare they were chasing? Bobby's story of his second encounter, when he was a full-grown man, seems to suggest the latter.

That time Bobby and his friends were chasing a particularly elusive hare. They became very exasperated before they finally cornered it. One of them, Tom Johnson, moved in to finish it off with a stick. Another, George Bell, stopped him.

'Let it be. T'would be a hanging affair if you killed it.' This suggests that the huntsmen had visions of a dead hare turning into a human corpse which would have to be explained to the Coroner. This was, incidentally, a first-hand account of the affair, told by Bobby himself in later life to Major J. Fairfax-Blakeborough, who, like his father Richard, was an enthusiastic witch-story hunter.

Alice Wood, known as 'Ailer,' who also operated in Bilsdale, was a very wily witch indeed. Not only was she reputed to turn herself into a hare but she managed on one occasion to slip out of a trap set for her as a human being. A local girl, Annie Wilson, was sure Ailer had bewitched her boy friend because the lad had taken up with another girl. (No-one, it seems, thought of accusing the new girl friend of witchcraft). Acting on the advice of Henry Wilson, the Broughton Wise Man, mentioned before, Annie took a four-legged stool, turned it upside down and stuck pins in its legs — three lots of nine new pins.

Then, Henry told her, she must get Ailer to sit on the stool. If she could contrive this, Ailer wouldn't be able to get up until she had confessed to bewitching Annie's faithless boy friend. So Annie invited Ailer to the house, offered her a cup of tea, saying, 'Sit here and drink your tea, Ailer.' Ailer refused. 'I'm not sitting on yon pricky-back 'otchen (i.e. hedgehog),' said she, pointing at the stool.

In Basedale lived another witch — Jane Wood. She was another who is said to have turned herself into a hare but she doesn't seem to have done anyone harm. Therefore it was, perhaps, rather unkind of a local sportsman to have taken aim at her with the usual silver shot in his gun. Afterwards she was found to have numerous small wounds in her rear. She explained that she'd accidentally overturned a bee-hive. Nobody believed her, of course.

We have already heard of witch activities in Stokesley but the first record of a Stokesley witch was nearly three hundred years ago. In an old diary appears the following:

'6th July 1699. Susan Ambler was whipped and put on the ducking stool (in Stokesley) for causing an evil spell on Adam Clark's sheep. He only got two score lambs and nine were black ones.'

Adam had to blame someone for a poor lambing season. Since it was in the time when witchcraft was a punishable offence, maybe Susan got off comparatively lightly. It may, of course, have been partly her own fault. Some reputed witches traded on their sinister reputations. They used a kind of blackmail. 'Give me what I want or suffer the consequences.' Then if some misfortune happened to the person, the witch would remind them of their non-

Stokesley, c.1846. Home of Mary Marshall and other witches. Photo reproduced by courtesy of Cleveland County Libraries from John Walker Ord's 'History of Cleveland' (1846).

cooperation. If nothing happened to them, nothing was said and the witch's threat was forgotten.

Much nearer our own time was Mary Marshall, described as 'nobbut an old meddling piece of nowt' by those living at the beginning of the 20th century who could recall her. She was said to bewitch crops, animals and people. A perfectly good cow could be reduced to an emaciated wreck by old Mary's ill-wishing. There is, however, one piece of witchcraft recorded of her where sympathy might well be with her rather than her victim.

A Stokesley man called Morton was known to have perjured himself in order to get his friend off a murder charge. He was on horseback when he met Mary Marshall one morning.

'Out of my way, spawn of the Devil,' says he.

Mary cast her eye on him. 'As you fall from your horse, you shall fall in fortune. As your horse runs, so shall your wealth.' The horse promptly threw Morton and galloped off. He never prospered from that day on.

Mary Marshall was paid out for her ill-wishing. It is said that she lost her wits, used to crow loudly every time she came upon hens or chickens. This was a direct result of her Devil-dealing — or so Stokesley folk believed.

The Wise Man of Stokesley, John Wrightson, was famous all over North Yorkshire in the late 18th and 19th centuries, though he cannot be identified for certain in official records. Much was, however, written about him. The writers show a decided difference of opinion about his character and abilities. Those writing about him during his lifetime and just after his death have little good to say of him. He was, they said, a charlatan, charging uneducated people high fees for worthless remedies and advice. He convinced some of them that their problems were the result of witchcraft, thus giving a bad reputation to harmless folk whom he labelled as witches.

On the other hand, those who had consulted him, telling of their experiences years later, had nothing but good to say of him. They respected his judgment and went in awe of his extraordinary powers. Canon Atkinson in his early days as Vicar of Danby talked to such people and they convinced him that Wrightson's bad reputation was entirely unjustified. The idea that he overcharged for his remedies was unlikely to be true, thought Canon Atkinson. He knew that Yorkshire country people are not the sort to pay out money without a fair return. Richard Blakeborough, who also obtained first-hand evidence of Wrightson's skills, was inclined to agree with him though he admitted that Wrightson probably 'dressed up' his advice and remedies to take account of the beliefs current in his day.

Wrightson's activities that have been recorded in this way are mostly to do with finding stolen property or curing illness in man and animals. The one story about him that concerns witchcraft has already been told in Chapter 3 because it is almost certain that the Wise Man consulted by Gawain Pierson's friend was John Wrightson. That story shows his uncanny power of knowing what his clients had come about before they opened their mouths.

The story of how John Wrightson came to the end of his days, however, fits in with the less favourable reports of his character. It is said that he left Stokesley and went to Malton where in 1818 he fell foul of the law, being committed to prison on a charge of fraud. He committed suicide before being brought to trial — or so it was claimed. However this final episode in his history was told in a newspaper report written 45 years after the event and no contemporary records have so far come to light to confirm the story.

Chapter Six

The law takes a hand at Thirsk and Helmsley

Since Thirsk and Helmsley were places where Justice was dispensed at the Quarter Sessions, it is not surprising that we find witches at both places recorded in 17th century documents. For example, the townsfolk of Thirsk decided to call in the Law over Elizabeth Cooke. She was a bad-tempered woman, always at odds with her neighbours (like Peggy Flounders of Marske, 200 years later). Elizabeth, however, was prosecuted as a witch. In July 1611, she was summoned to answer the following indictment:

'Elizabeth, wife of John Cooke of Thirsk, for a common scold and disquieter of her neighbours with continual banning and cursing of her neighbours and their goods inasmuch as the said goods and themselves whom she curseth oftentimes presently die (as they verily think) by her said evil words.'

This was in the reign of James I when the law was strict against any form of witchcraft. The king himself believed that witches possessed supernatural powers though he modified his views on witch-trials later in his reign, being suspicious of the kind of evidence brought against reputed witches. The Justices at Thirsk felt that the case against Elizabeth Cooke wasn't proven. Her neighbours were taking her curses a great deal too seriously, they thought. After all, quarrels between neighbours were common enough and many people said more than they meant when they were in a temper. The words 'as they verily think' seem to suggest that the official recorder, too, had his doubts as to whether Elizabeth's curses really produced the death of men and beasts. The case appears to have been dismissed. Thirsk Parish Register records the burial of an Elizabeth Cooke, widow, in 1631, so it seems likely that Thirsk put up with her for another 20 years.

On the other hand, only 12 years later, another Elizabeth didn't get off so lightly. In October 1623 Elizabeth, wife of Thomas Creary of Northallerton, was accused of:

'exercising certain most wicked arts, enchantments and charms on a black cow (value 50 shillings) belonging to Edward Bell of Northallerton by which the cow was sorely damaged and the calf within her totally wasted and consumed.'

Was it because this was a specific piece of damage to a valuable piece of property brought about by Elizabeth's witchcraft or was it that Farmer Bell had given the prosecution so much information that they could hardly overlook it? Whatever the reason, Elizabeth was convicted and sentenced 'to be set in the pillory, once a quarter, in some market town in the Riding upon some Fair or Market Day.'

If after four sessions in the pillory, she remained of good behaviour, the Justices considered that Elizabeth had atoned for her crime. No doubt she kept well away from Edward Bell and his livestock after that.

Elizabeth seems to have been the only witch punished that way in the North Riding Quarter Sessions records, but in Lancashire, where witches suffered a good deal more than in Yorkshire, there was a similar case. Margaret Pearson was convicted of killing a horse by witchcraft and had to stand in the pillory every three months for a year.

North Yorkshire didn't prosecute many witches, though. There were only six cases involving witchcraft in the Quarter Sessions records between 1606 and 1657 and none at all after that date. The 17th century was a time when witch trials were extremely common over most of England, so Yorkshire Justices appear to have been tolerant, or perhaps enlightened. Perhaps, like James I, they realised that damage to life and property caused by witchcraft is extremely difficult to prove, even if you believe that such damage can be caused.

There are records of other courts where witches were put on trial. Some time between January and March 1649 (the year is sometimes written as 1650 because the Julian Calendar was in use then and its year began in March), Isaac Newton of Bagdale Hall, Whitby, was called upon to try a witch. This witch, William Mason, belonged to the village of Old Byland and he had been doing some very odd things.

Cromwell was in control of England at the time and a detachment of his army was encamped near William's home. William was said to have caused the apparition of a woman to appear at the bedside of his brother Robert. Robert didn't complain but one William Kirkham of Rievaulx had some very searching questions to ask about the affair. He asked Mason, 'How did you dare to do this and many other strange matters amongst the soldiery? They might have fallen on you and killed you.'

Mason was quite unrepentant and very confident about his supernatural powers. 'I had them fixed so that they had no power to pistol, stab, kill or cut me,' he replied. This was as good as a confession. Kirkham told the man, 'I believe that, for this offensive behaviour of yours, the justices will send you to prison or to a House of Correction.'

Mason was not intimidated in the least.

'If so, I will make some follow me and when they are fast, I shall go out at my pleasure.'

You will notice that the supernatural element in the affair was being played down. As we have seen, it is difficult to get evidence on witchcraft activities. Kirkham changed his tactics.

'Do you think we shall have a King in England?' he asked. This was only months after the execution of Charles I so if Mason answered 'yes' he would be confessing to having Royalist sympathies. However, Mason didn't worry about that. He replied, 'I'll warrant you there shall be a King and that very shortly."

There is absolutely no record of what happened to William Mason, the witch. Were his powers sufficient to keep him from being convicted? Or was Cromwell's influence not quite so strong in North Yorkshire as it was elsewhere?

There was another case of witchcraft in the Helmsley records, also during the time of Cromwell's power. This time the defendant was a member of the upper classes. In January 1657 Rob Conyers, gentleman, late of Guisborough, was summoned to appear at Helmsley charged with 'certain detestable arts of sorcery, wickedly to practise the same.'

He is said to have got off with a fine. There is some evidence to suggest that Rob Conyers mended his ways because a Robert Conyers appears in the Jury List at Helmsley on two occasions between 1657 and 1716. Jurymen are chosen from those who are 'good men and true.'

Unfortunately, we can't be sure. There is more than one Robert Conyers in 17th century records of this part of North Yorkshire. There is one at Guisborough, but he was there after Rob the Wizard appeared in court at Helmsley. Leonard Conyers, of Bagdale Hall, Whitby, who died in 1595 had a son called Robert, one of a large family, not his father's heir. Rob Conyers is a bit of a mystery.

Perhaps a more intriguing mystery is what Rob Conyers was up to in 1657 that Helmsley Justices found so detestable. Since he was a gentleman — a man of independant means — he would hardly be trying to make a living by fortune-telling like Ralph Milner of Muker (more of him in chapter 7). It is possible that he was amusing himself by conducting scientific experiments ahead of his time. The Oxford mathematician Thomas Allen, who died in 1632, was reputed to deal in the Black Arts because he possessed a very unusual clock. His servants vowed that there was a devil inside it. Any piece of advanced technology was suspect in the days when even educated men believed in witchcraft.

There was a remarkable piece of advanced technology, or so it appeared, at Sowerby in the early 19th century. It was the property of the Wise Man of that town. The story about it does not concern witches — it was employed to catch thieves, a business over which many people consulted their local Wise Man. It was certainly regarded as being of a magical nature and perhaps should be included here.

The device was a crystal, about the size of a goose's egg. It seemed to work rather like the modern closed-circuit TV set. Two men from Brompton (a village about 1½ miles north-east of Northallerton) arrived at Sowerby to consult the Wise Man on behalf of their friend, Mark Jopling, a weaver. Mark had had a break-in at his workshop. Valuable cloth and tools had been stolen. The Wise Man produced his crystal and invited the Brompton men to look into it and see what it told them. They could see nothing. This, said the Wise Man, was because neither of them had been born under the right planet. Fortunately, he told them, he knew of a lad who had been born under the right planet and he would (for a small fee) look into the crystal for them.

It was truly astonishing what the lad could see. There was Mark Jopling's workshop, there were the thieves making their getaway. The crystal kept them in view as they travelled to Yarm, then on to South Stockton (Thornaby-on-Tees) where they booked in at a public house. The crystal must have been equipped with sound recording because the lad could hear them talking. They would stay at the pub until 8 a.m. the following morning.

'Now's your chance,' the Wise Man told his clients. 'Go after them and catch them red-handed.' The men set off on horseback and reached South Stockton in record time. There they had a problem. South Stockton had three pubs and they had forgotten to find out from the magic glass expert which one the thieves had booked into. By the time they'd tried all three, it was too late to catch the thieves. Bad luck on all concerned — except for the Wise Man and his assistant who, no doubt, had asked for cash in advance.

The little village of Nunnington had a witch in the 1840's. Local farmers believed that she had taken a cow's heart, stuck it full of pins and said a 'foul nominy' (an evil rhyme or jingle) over it, while burning it in a fire. Afterwards several cows had died and when the owners cut the beasts open, they found one of them had pin-holes in its heart. This was evidence of a witch at work. So the locals decided to consult a Wise Woman nearby and ask her to identify the witch responsible.

When this came to the ears of the Vicar, Rev. William Keary, he was greatly distressed to find such superstitious beliefs were abroad in his parish. He assumed that the would-be witch hunters were the less educated members of his flock. He had a quiet word with one of the older members of the community, a gentleman of some influence and a regular church-goer. 'Can you persuade them to give up the idea of going to this Wise Woman?' he asked. 'It will have more effect coming from you.' He was horrified to discover that it was the older members of the community who had thought of the idea in the first place. What was he to do? All he could think of was to preach a sermon against the un-Christian practice of believing in witches and of accusing fellow villagers of causing harm by witchcraft.

Needless to say, Rev. William Keary was extremely unpopular that Sunday. John Peacock, the senior member of the church, referred to earlier, called at the Vicarage and very politely but firmly spoke his mind.

'We're maybe very wise, parson,' he said. 'I knows you're learned, but in this matter you knows nowt whatever and you're altogether mistaken. I can't go against what I see'd with my own eyes.'

We do not know how the story ended. We only know it happened because Mr. Keary's daughter, Annie (who later became quite a well-known writer), described the incident in her memoirs. She seems to have sided with old John Peacock. 'John had the best of the argument,' she wrote. 'He spoke from experience, my father only spoke from opinion.'

Strange things do happen, even in these days. Is it wiser to speak from experience than from opinion? No doubt, John Peacock and his friends wouldn't know as much about diseases to which a cow can fall victim as, for example, our Yorkshire vet James Herriot knows in these days. On the other hand, Mr. Herriot would be the first to admit that neither he nor his colleagues know everything.

Chapter Seven

Wizards and Witches in Richmondshire

The little village of Brignall, four miles south-east of Barnard Castle, was the home of a would-be wizard over 400 years ago. He was John Phillip, whose family had property near Brignall in 1575. It seems that John had a wicked uncle, James, who had grabbed the property from his older brother, Charles, when their father died. Charles was John's father.

John appears to have been very bitter at the loss of his inheritance. He resolved to lay a curse on his uncle's family. The magical ingredients of this curse were taken from a book on occult philosophy by Cornelius Agrippa of Netteshein, published on the Continent in 1532. John copied the magical symbols from Agrippa's book onto a couple of sheets of lead.

Then he added the curse:

'I do make this that James Phillip, John Phillip, his son, Christopher Phillip and Thomas Phillip, his sons, shall fly Richmondshire and nothing prosper with any of them in Richmondshire. I did make this that the father, James Phillip, John Phillip and all kin of Phillip and all issue of them shall come presently to utter beggary and nothing joy or prosper with them in Richmondshire.' Signed J. Phillip.

John Phillip hid his leaden tablets away. He doesn't seem to have told anyone about them and we don't know whether he tried any other experiment with magic. We would not have known anything about John and his would-be wizardry had not the tablets come to light 200 years later. In 1789, a William Hawkesworth was investigating a tumulus (ancient burial ground) close to the old Roman road where it crosses Gatherley Moor near Middleton Tyas. He came upon the leaden tablets and was intrigued by the curse.

Who was this John Phillip? He consulted a Mr. John C. Brooke, a member of the College of Heralds who had access to the family trees of landed gentry. Sure enough, Mr. Brooke identified the Phillip family, their names corresponding very closely with those named in the curse.

When he examined the records, Mr. Brooke found that James Phillip had taken over the Brignall property, although his brother Charles was the elder. He also found that James's family had not prospered, the estate falling into other hands after a few years. So it appears that the curse had worked. However, the same records revealed that John Phillip and his family hadn't done very well either which might serve as a warning to anyone else who might be tempted to use occult magic as a means of getting their own back on a wicked uncle. Perhaps John should have been more careful with the wording of his curse. The phrase 'all kin of Phillip' might well apply to himself and, as we have seen in the case of the Wise Man, Henry Wilson, magic workers were warned against the possibility of a counter spell being turned against the person who cast it if the supposed evil doer was innocent.

There have been doubts expressed as to the authenticity of the Brignall tablets. Mrs. Gutch, who recorded their discovery at the beginning of the 20th century for the Yorkshire Folklore Society, pointed out that there were names

No. i. Obverse.

No. i, Reverse.

No. ii. Obverse.

No. ii. Reverse.

The Brignall Tablets, originally published in 'Examples of Printed Folklore concerning the North Riding' by Mrs. Gutch (1899).

in the Phillip family tree that don't appear in the curse. This could be accounted for if we imagine that John hadn't anything against them, or that they had died before he wrote his curse. Mrs. Gutch also noted that Cornelius Agrippa's book wasn't published in England until 1651 whereas the inheritance that caused John such offence must have passed into his uncle's hands more than half a century earlier. However, John Phillip could surely have obtained his copy from a continental bookseller. Young men of good family frequently visited France and Germany in those days.

Whether the Brignall curse was genuine or not, there was certainly another Richmondshire wizard practising the Forbidden Arts in 1606. Ralph Milner, a

'Witch charms' (a string of stones with holes through them). The originals are in the Ryedale Folk Museum. Photo by T. Middlemass, courtesy of the Crosland Foundation.

yeoman (small land-owner) of Rashe, appeared before Richmond Quarter Sessions on 13th October 1606 'being accused of sorcery, witchcraft, enchantment, and telling of fortunes.'

Unlike Rob Conyers, he wasn't merely let off with a fine. He was ordered to: 'Make his submission at Mewcarr (Muker) church upon Sunday next in time of Divine Service and confess that he hath highly offended God and deluded man and is heartily sorry and will offend no more.'

The interesting thing about his sentence, as recorded by the Sessions clerk, is that his behaviour is condemned as 'deluding man,' in other words pretending to be able to foretell the future, very much the same as later courts convicted fortune-tellers as cheating the customers who paid for what they genuinely believed was a look into the future. Yet this was at a time when even educated men believed that witches really were in league with the Devil. Yorkshire Justices do seem to have been very enlightened men.

No further reference to Ralph Milner's activities as a sorcerer appears in the Quarter Sessions records so it must be assumed that he complied with the Court Order. However the name of Ralph Milner appears seven years later, as being fined 2s. 6d. for his 'abuse in court.' It may not be the same individual, of course. There was a number of Ralph Milners in the Richmond area during the 17th century but it does rather suggest that Ralph the Wizard may still have been crossing swords with the law.

Belief in witchcraft lingered into the 19th century in this area of North Yorkshire, as it did in Whitby and Goathland. There was a reputed witch in Catterick at the time when folk lore researchers were collecting material, the date given being around the 1850's. An elderly lady interviewed by Margaret Gatty had a string of 'lucky stones' hanging behind the door of her house. These were stones with holes through their centres (Ryedale Folk Museum has some similar). She told Margaret Gatty these were very important to her. She needed them to protect her from a certain person in Catterick who possessed the Evil Eye and had caused the death of a young girl by that means, the lass having fallen ill of 'a pining sickness.'

Old Sally Kindreth of Scorton, active 1800 to 1810, was believed to have cast spells on those she didn't like. By all accounts she had some excuse for it. Poor Sally was a cripple. A weaver's beam had fallen on her when she was a young girl, leaving her with a twisted back. The younger generation wasn't very kind to the poor old soul.

One day, a crowd of lads was tormenting her. They'd dragged her to the banks of the Swale and were about to heave her into the water when a stranger came by. It's a pity we don't know his name because his heart was in the right place.

'Let the old dame go and I'll fight the best man among you,' was his offer. The ring-leader, George Pennock, took up the challenge .He got the worse of the fight. As so often happens, the rest of the gang weren't very upset at his defeat. George was a handsome enough specimen but had a bad reputation. After he picked himself up, Sally had the last word.

'My curse on him for doing evil,' she told the crowd. 'There are more seeds in a poppy-head than there are days left for him to live. He'll die with his head under water but he won't die of drowning.'

Not long afterwards, a young married couple, Tom and Polly Kaye, set out to visit Polly's mother who lived at Bolton-on-Swale. They didn't return home at the time their friends expected them to arrive. After a long wait, those friends became suspicious that something had happened to Tom and Polly. William Boddy, the local cobbler, had a reputation for being something of a Wise Man. Like the Wise Man of Sowerby, he had a magic device that acted like a TV set. This time it was said to have been a fragment of glass from one of the old Abbeys, Easby or Jervaux, rescued after the Dissolution.

William looked into his magic glass, and had a dramatic story to tell from it. There were Tom and Polly, walking home by the banks of the Swale. There was George Pennock creeping up behind them. George hit Tom over the head and grabbed Polly. Delicacy prevented the telling of what the infamous George did next (this story was recorded in Victorian times, of course), but William Boddy could see it all too clearly.

A search party set out immediately. On the river bank they found Tom, unconscious, but there was no sign of Polly, or her abductor. William Boddy's magic could help no further, so Sally Kindreth was called in. She took a loaf of bread and some coins that Polly was known to have handled. These she rubbed with quicksilver (i.e. mercury), thrust them into the loaf and threw it into the Swale at the spot where Tom had been found. It floated downstream; they followed it until it came to rest by the bank. Polly's body was found close by.

The law was called in, a warrant was issued for George's arrest but he had a fast horse and escaped. Tom recovered from his injuries but there was only one idea in his head — to find the man who had murdered and dishonoured his wife. Tom was a waggoner so his occupation helped him in his search. Sally Kindreth told him, 'You'll not catch him, but he'll be found at the end of fifteen round ones' (i.e. fifteen months).

Sally was right. In early October, the year following Polly's murder, Tom was in the Salutation Inn at Leeming near Bedale with a group of other waggoners. It was a night of storm, the waggoners thankful they had a good roof over them. The wind drowned all other sounds from outside the inn. Then came a sound like the yelping of dogs and the waggoners shivered. 'The gabby ratch! (Gabriel's hounds)' they said. No-one would have put a step outside the inn after hearing that dreadful sound. It heralded death for someone. If there was a faint cry for help mixed in with that supernatural yelping, no-one would have dared to enquire.

Some time later a stable lad came running in. He'd gone to the horse trough and there was a corpse lying in it, face downwards. It was brought into the inn and Tom saw — the dead man was George Pennock. He'd been stabbed in the back and had fallen into the trough as he died. Tom heaved a sigh of relief.

'If I'd found him, there would still have been murder done. Polly is revenged but my hands are clean.'

George's murderer was never found. Old Sally ended her days in Lancashire with her married niece. Did she know who killed George? Who can tell?

Chapter Eight

Devil at work in the Dales

As we have seen, in the days when witchcraft was a punishable offence, North Yorkshire Justices were often reluctant to convict witches. There are, in fact, a couple of cases in 17th century court records that show the law called upon to defend a supposed witch. In 1640 a New Malton mason and his wife were in trouble for 'uttering scandalous words against Elizabeth England by saying she was a witch and they would prove her one.'

In 1691 at Bedale, Timothy Wainde, late of Friby, yeoman, appeared in court for 'uttering false and scandalous words to the defamation of Alice Boville; to wit "Thou bewitchest my stot"' (i.e. young ox). Timothy, a yeoman farmer, would be a man of some consequence in the district and we don't know whether Alice was anybody of greater consequence than an ordinary member of the village community. She probably wasn't a housewife or the name of her husband would surely have been mentioned, as was the custom. But it is interesting to note that it was her reputation that the law was being asked to defend, at a time when any accusation of witchcraft was taken very seriously indeed.

A century later, there were still accusations of witchcraft going about in the Bedale area. This particular area of the Dales appears to have needed two Wise Men to help cope with them. These were Master Sadler and Thomas Spence. We know that Master Sadler was in practice as a Wise Man in 1773 because he advertised his services that year, undertaking to cure 'ague' (shivering fits, often due to a form of malaria) by writing the sufferer's name on the back of his fireplace and reciting a special incantation. Records suggest that Thomas Spence lived at Pond House, Bedale, in 1731.

Both of these gentlemen were called in to deal with the notorious Molly Cass, who lived near the mill at Leeming and was always causing trouble.

This particular piece of trouble concerned Jane Herd's caul. A caul is a piece of thin membrane sometimes found covering the face of a new-born baby. In times past, it was thought very lucky to have been born with a caul over your face. Mothers always kept this membrane very carefully, often giving it to the child when he or she was grown up. It was believed to be full of magical powers that could be used for good or evil.

Jane had been born with a caul and could do wonderful things with it. For example, if she particularly wanted to see a friend or relative, she had only to lay the caul on her Bible, say their name and the person was sure to arrive at the door in a very short time. Extremely handy in days when there was neither telephone nor telegraph service. Jane was, however, a good-living girl who only used her caul for harmless magic like this.

One day, when Jane was using it to 'call up' a friend, a puff of wind blew it out of the open window. Jane ran outside at once but couldn't find it anywhere. After that, everything seemed to go wrong for poor Jane. Her boy friend lost interest in her and she developed a huge swelling on her neck, another on her knee. It was quite plain to Jane and her family that someone had found that caul and was using it to work evil against its owner. So Messrs. Sadler and Spence were called in.

They boiled certain smelly ingredients in a saucepan over a fire of rowan wood. Jane was told she had to inhale the fumes. Then, Bible in hand, she had to think of all the people who could possibly have taken possession of that caul and say each name aloud. As she did so, the Wise Men kept their eyes on the saucepan. Jane said several names but at each one, the saucepan didn't respond and the Wise Men pronounced, 'No, she is free!'

Then Jane named Molly Cass. Immediately, the saucepan boiled over, the room was filled with evil-smelling fumes and everyone was forced to go outside. There they found Molly Cass, peeping in at the window. They seized her, thrust her into the fume-filled kitchen and refused to let her out until she confessed to having taken Jane's caul. Next day, Molly was ducked nine times in Bedale mill dam. After that, no doubt, Jane got her caul back.

Molly Cass had everyone scared of her. There were those who vowed they'd seen her flying along on her broomstick near Leeming Mill where she lived in a tumbledown little cottage. Whether you believe that or not, there were some odd things going on in that cottage and those who remembered her, telling about it in the middle of the 19th century, were quite sure that she had some very uncanny powers.

Three local men, Willie Cummins, Tommy Horner and James Poulter, seem to have been less scared of her than most because when the three of them had an argument about which of them owned a certain cow, they called on Molly to arbitrate. Molly told them to go away home. 'A turnip's settled it,' she said. Puzzled, the men did as she told them. They found that the cow had choked over a turnip and was lying dead in the cow byre.

There was a certain George Winterfield in Leeming who had got a girl pregnant and wasn't prepared to marry her. Molly appeared one night as he was playing cards with his mates.

'The auld 'un (the devil) is in thee now, George,' she told him. 'He'll not leave thee until he's gotten thee for good.'

George was terrified, so great was her reputation. 'I'll wed the lass,' he promised. 'Give us one more chance, Molly. I'll make an honest woman of her.' Molly shook her head. 'Ah seldom give folk one chance, let lone two,' she replied. 'The girl's waiting for thee, George. She's asleep in the bulrushes. Go to her. All roads lead to the Swale tonight.'

George stumbled through the door, muttering that he'd go and see the girl straight away. His friends never saw him again. No-one knew exactly what happened to him that night, whether he lost his way in the dark or whether something more sinister happened. They found his body in the Swale next morning. Not far from it was another corpse — that of the girl he'd refused to marry. She had thrown herself into the river, rather than face the shame of having a 'base-begotten' child.

How far was Molly responsible for what happened to George? Did she know about the suicide and use her special powers to see that George suffered for it? Was the girl somebody Molly liked, could she even have been a close relative?

Unfortunately there is no independent record of this double tragedy, nor trace of George in the parish registers for the area.

North of Bedale is the village of Hornby where Mother Webster lived, though we have no date for her activities. It is difficult to be sure whether she was a true witch, though she dealt in magic spells. Squire Hewgill consulted her once. Like the squire of Anngrove and the Goathland landowner, he had a daughter determined to marry a man not of her father's choosing. He locked her up in her room, of course, but when that didn't make her change her mind he asked Mother Webster for a charm that would change it for her. Mother Webster was against the idea. 'Let them marry,' was her advice. Squire Hewgill persisted and in the end she prescribed a 'do it yourself' charm like Nanny of Ayton gave Johnny Simpson (chapter 5).

An extraordinary feature of this charm was that Hewgill was told to say a prayer to St. Agnes at one point in the charm weaving. You wouldn't think a saint would be likely to help in the devil's work, would you? Perhaps that is what made things go badly wrong. After Squire Hewgill had finished and was on his way home, a weasel ran across his path. This, Mother Webster told him, would cancel the charm. Whether it did or not will never be known because Hewgill's unfortunate daughter, realising that her father would never give his consent to her marriage, committed suicide and Hewgill was haunted by her ghost for the rest of his life.

To the south of Bedale, in Carthorpe, Dolly Ayre gave her neighbours a lot of trouble. She cast a spell on old Tommy's cows and refused to take it off. Another Wise Man came to the rescue. He was Sammy Banks of Mickley and the witch-story hunter, Richard Blakeborough, had a first-hand account of what happened, even if the details were a little vague. Sammy 'burnt summat that stank worse than owt.' Tommy lost one cow but the others recovered — thanks to Mr. Banks.

Dolly Ayre couldn't even be kind to those who were kind to her. A family did her a good turn once but when they moved house she ill-wished the place. Shortly after they moved in, a heavy wooden shelf collapsed killing a child who was standing underneath it. Dolly's fault, said the neighbours. Kindness did no good when you dealt with a Bedale witch but it seems to have worked wonders with the witches of Staithes (see chapter 2).

In the Dales there were a couple of witches who had no fixed abode. They went about the countryside selling small articles. Old Mother Stebbins was one of them, Dolly Machin the other. Old Dolly had an astonishing reputation. Richard Blakeborough was told that she once travelled from the top of Ingleborough to Great Whernside in a single leap. He found it a little hard to believe, and said so to the old lady who told him the tale. She was a little put out at his disbelief, then said to him, 'Don't you want her to have done it?' Perhaps that is why we have so many witch stories. We are a little sceptical but we want them to have done it. Perhaps we in this supersonic age can be a little more credulous of a leap that spanned nine miles or so.

Lastly there was Bessy Slack of West Burton in Wensleydale. Little is known of her deeds except that there were families in West Burton who, when a new baby was expected, always kept the cradle it was to occupy upside down until the child was actually born and ready to be placed in it. In this way, they believed, Bessy or any other witch who happened to be around, couldn't harm the new-comer with an ante-natal spell.

Chapter Nine

Witches accused around Ripon

Kirkby Malzeard, seven miles north-west of Ripon, had a number of Wise Men and Wise Women in the 17th century who claimed they could cure a whole range of ailments, from ear-ache to heart-ache. One of them had a try at curing insomnia which unfortunately got her into trouble.

On December 16th 1639, Janet Burniston was called before a special court held at Kirkby Malzeard church. She was accused of having removed a skull from the graveyard and taken it home with her. Skulls were well-known ingredients of spells and charms. The juices surrounding a decaying skull were used in Scotland to make 'dead bree,' an antidote against illness in cattle brought on by witchcraft.

Janet was very honest with the court. She explained that she intended to put the skull under the head of one, Christopher, in order to 'charm him asleep.' Whether this was simply a case of trying to help Christopher to get a good night's rest or whether the word 'asleep' had a more sinister meaning, isn't very clear. However the court must have decided that Janet meant Christopher no harm by her action because they merely told her to put the skull back where she found it. Considering that this incident happened at a time when even well-meaning witchcraft carried a heavy penalty, Janet was exceptionally lucky, though, as we have seen, North Yorkshire justices were reluctant to convict witches.

It was 15 years after this incident that a very different witchcraft case came up at Studley Hall, near Ripon. This was the home of Sir John Mallory, M.P. for Ripon. He had been a prominent Royalist during the Civil War but seems to have coped with the change to Commonwealth rule without losing either property or prestige. He had a 14-year-old daughter, Elizabeth, who was at the centre of the trouble.

Near Studley Hall lived a married couple, Mary and William Wade. Elizabeth doesn't seem to have known them particularly well. She had visited their cottage with her mother, and Mrs. Wade had offered her guests a little refreshment — a dish of nuts. She'd met Mrs. Wade in the milk-house at Studley Hall on one occasion and Mrs. Wade had begged her to give her a piece of bread. This was rather surprising because the Wades weren't poor people. There seemed no reason for Mary Wade to have begged for something to eat. Indeed, Mary made a joke of it, saying that she'd heard the bread at Studley Hall to be of exceptionally high quality and she had a fancy to taste it.

These minor incidents were brought out at the trial because there was a strong belief in those days that if you gave or received food from a witch it somehow gave the witch power over you. A trial there was, because, not long afterwards, Elizabeth Mallory fell ill. She lost the use of her limbs and became subject to strange fits of trembling. The girl seemed to know when these fits were going to happen because she would warn those about her that she was going to be ill.

This went on for several months. Elizabeth stayed in bed, unable to move without help. Then, when she was having one of her trembling fits, Elizabeth suddenly screamed out 'She comes! Mary comes!' A servant whose job it was to wait on the sick girl tried to find out who this 'Mary' was that was causing Elizabeth so much distress. The christian name was a common one then, as now. All Elizabeth would say was 'Mary comes!' So the servant went through the names of all the women called Mary that she could think of. When she got to 'Mary Wade' Elizabeth screamed and cried with fright so, of course, it looked as if Mary Wade was responsible.

After the fit was over, Elizabeth told her mother that she was sure Mary Wade had cast a spell on her, but if Mary was to come and confess and beg her pardon, she was sure that she would be well. So Lady Mallory sent for Mary Wade and asked her to do what Elizabeth wanted. Not surprisingly, Mary Wade didn't want to do it. She had no desire to confess to being a witch. Lady Mallory persisted, saying that it might help Elizabeth if she did. In the end, Mary agreed, went to Elizabeth's bedroom and said what was required. Immediately Elizabeth was able to get out of bed and announced that she was cured.

Unfortunately, Mary, not wanting to get a reputation for witchcraft, privately assured Lady Mallory and the other members of the household that she hadn't cast any spell at all. Of course this got to Elizabeth's ears. 'If she denies it, I shall be ill again!' Elizabeth declared and sure enough the trembling fits started all over again.

Then it was William Wade's turn to become involved. Elizabeth took to crying out, 'William, thou terrifier!' in her bouts of sickness. She started to have bouts of vomiting and out of her mouth came a whole mass of pins — another sign of a witchcraft-induced illness. William was sent for and asked to confess, to beg Elizabeth's pardon. He was not quite so obliging as his wife and firmly told Lady Mallory that although he believed Elizabeth was possessed by an evil spirit which was causing her illness he wasn't responsible for it in any way.

It seems strange to us in these days, but the Mallorys were firmly convinced that Elizabeth had been bewitched by Mary and William Wade. The two were arrested and put in jail. The case was tried at York and all the details were duly recorded by court officials. It was also recorded that 'after she (Elizabeth) was assured that they were both in hold (i.e. prison) she was freed from her fits and so continued for about a fortnight.'

There is no record of what the court decided after the hearing was over. The Justices might well have had their doubts about the whole accusation. It was not unknown for young people to pretend to be ill and claim that someone had bewitched them. There had been a similar case at York in 1622 when a group of Knaresborough women had been accused of bewitching Maud Jeffray and two other children, daughters of Edward Fairfax. These women had had very sinister reputations according to their neighbours — possessing strange animals, believed to be familiar spirits, trading on their reputation as witches to get money and food from their neighbours. Nevertheless, after the judges at York had cross-questioned the children, it was revealed that the whole thing had been pretence on their part. John Jeffray, Maud's father, had some grudge against the women, had encouraged Maud to pretend illness and the Fairfax children had joined in, as children will do sometimes. Jeffray was sent to prison for fraud. With this case in mind it is not surprising that the York judges were suspicious that the case against Mary and William was based on a similar pretence by Mistress Elizabeth Mallory, for reasons best known to herself.

However, there was one Ripon witch who came to a bad end, or so the story goes. Mr. Fairfax Blakeborough found evidence of it in an early 19th century manuscript written by David Naitby, Bedale schoolmaster, and a man called Hird.

'Mary Milner of Ripon this day Friday 1st June 1821 did tell me (she having good memory of it) that in April 1764 (she in her 10th year) one, Master Ogle, who did commonly smell witches, on that day smelled one to her death.'

This is a most extraordinary case. There were, of course, 'witch-finders' in the 17th century though we have no evidence that any of them put their noses over the Yorkshire border. Master Ogle's activities took place 28 years after the laws against witchcraft were repealed so his witch cannot have met her death at the hands of the law. However public opinion and legal opinion didn't always go hand in hand. This Ripon witch may very likely have met her end by mob violence but we have only Mary Milner's word for what occurred.

Last of all in the Ripon area was Nanny Appleby who lived somewhere on Dalton Moor. A widow living in Aldfield had a son seriously ill. Nanny was called in and said the lad was possessed with a devil. She drove the devil out to the accompaniment of shrieks and much smashing of crockery. Then she commanded the devil to enter the body of someone else — she being unable, it seems, to send the devil back to where it belonged. The devil promptly entered the body of a lad called Tom Moss (whom Nanny didn't like much) and he was found drowned a month later. The widow's son made a complete recovery.

Chapter Ten

Other Yorkshire Witches

This book is about the witches who lived in North Yorkshire but it must not be thought that the rest of the County of York was witch-less. Far from it. In fact, stories about witches in the south of Yorkshire have been included in a great many books on the subject so perhaps one or two of them should be included here for the purpose of comparison.

Apart from that one incident at Ripon, mentioned in the last chapter, no North Yorkshire witch seems to have lost her life because of her activities. However Pocklington was not so gentle with its witches. Their parish registers in the 17th century tell a sad story:

'3rd March 1630. Old wife Green burnt in market-place for a witch.

'4th March 1642. Petronel Haxley, the smith's wife, executed in the market-place for a witch.'

Petronel wasn't Pocklington's last witch, it seems. A year later the record reads:

'24th March 1643. Thomas Dobson, bewitched, buried.'

There was also the infamous Isabella of Pocklington and her husband. They were both executed at York in 1649 convicted of having crucified Isabella's mother as an act of Devil worship.

The case of old wife Green needs a little explanation. In England, when witches were put to death, they were hanged, not burnt. However the story goes that old wife Green came to her end, not by the action of the Law, but because an angry mob of townsfolk took matters into their own hands before they could be restrained.

Ann Wilkinson of Alne (3½ miles south of Easingwold) was accused of witchcraft at York, like Mary and William Wade. The case came up in 1670 but the jury didn't convict her. She was alleged to have put a spell upon a neighbour but at the very moment that her supposed victim was writhing in pain, a couple of other neighbours entered Ann's cottage unannounced, in the hope of catching her red-handed. They found Ann sitting quietly by the fire, minding her own business, not stirring smelly ingredients in a saucepan or reciting charms. This seems to have satisfied all concerned that Ann was innocent. Fortunately no-one thought of the possibility of a delayed action spell, completed before the would-be witnesses entered the cottage.

Old Tit Poole of Staveley achieved something that no North Yorkshire witch seems to have done. She was so well known that a road was named after her — Tit Poole's Lane. Sally Carey, a late 18th century witch who lived at Kirby Hill near Boroughbridge, was a thoroughly heartless character. One story told of her is about a trick even worse than that played by Nan Hardwick on the young farmer whose wife was about to give birth to their child (see chapter 4).

Sally quarrelled with a young married couple expecting their first child and said she'd see to it that the baby was a girl when the parents were desperately anxious for a boy. The baby did turn out to be a girl but that didn't satisfy Sally. The poor wife was plagued by Sally's threats and taunts even when her husband had been killed in a riding accident, a few weeks before their second child was due to be born. This time the baby was a boy but he was born with a disability — unable to walk normally when a toddler. The mother was told that her son would outgrow his disability but only if she did not remarry until the child was grown up. Sally did her best to spoil things again — the widow was constantly having to say 'no' to offers of marriage, apparently the result of Sally's efforts as a match-maker. Sally was defeated in the end but what a lot of heart-ache she'd caused.

Mary Bateman, who lived at the end of the 18th century, was a native of Topcliffe but her witch activities took place when she lived at Leeds. She made the mistake of using poison as well as charms to dispatch her victims and was eventually tried, condemned and hanged for murder at York on 20th March 1809. She died for murder but many who watched the execution (held in public then) weren't really easy in their minds until she was pronounced dead. They felt that her witchcraft might have been used to enable her to escape.

Knaresborough, as well as being the home of the alleged witches mentioned in chapter 9, was the birthplace of Ursula Shipton née Southeil, better known as Mother Shipton, the most famous witch in England. No fewer than 41 books have been written about her and her famous prophecies. No 20th century writer on folk lore or witchcraft ever fails to give her a mention. She is believed to have lived between 1488 and 1561 but at the beginning of this century there were quite a lot of people who classed her as a 'legendary figure' like King Arthur — probably having no real place in history at all.

The unfortunate thing about her history is that nothing was published about her or her prophecies until nearly 100 years after her death, and one of her earliest biographers, Richard Head, whose 'Life of Mother Shipton' was published in 1684, had the reputation of not sticking to known facts in his writings. Her prophecies too cannot all be ones she actually made herself. Later prophets are known to have written their own forecasts under her name — people would take more heed of them that way.

Neither is there a lot of evidence that her more famous predictions — the invention of the telegraph and the steam engine — appeared in print before the inventions themselves. Certainly one of the prophecies attributed to her was wide of the mark. According to Mother Shipton, the world should have come to an end in 1881.

Nevertheless, Mother Shipton seems to have been the only witch with a completely good reputation. No evil deed has ever been recorded as being her doing. Like Hannah Waugh of Broughton (chapter 5), Mother Shipton's magic was always directed against people who deserved it — never the weak or under-privileged members of society. Recently it has been suggested that the reason Mother Shipton never seems to have suffered at the hands of the Law was that she really had supernatural powers and the Law kept clear of her on that account.

In Conclusion

These were the witches of North Yorkshire. Had they really supernatural powers, able to change themselves into the shape of a hare, to ride through the night on a broomstick, to cause sickness and death by reciting charms or with a flash of their Evil Eye? Our ancestors certainly thought they had.

To us in the 20th century, some of the stories seem to have a perfectly natural explanation, if we care to look for it, but you mightn't have been able to convince our ancestors of this. After all, just suppose an 18th century Yorkshire man or woman was to come back to earth today and watch us as we pick up a piece of plastic, press a few buttons then speak to someone on the other side of the world as easily as if we were in the same room with him or her; he or she would certainly put the whole business down to witchcraft. It would be easier for our ancestors to believe that an old woman could fly through the air on a broomstick than that a hundred or more people could do the same in a metal container shaped like a bird.

Many of the witches believed in their own powers, that seems certain. There were, however, those who had no wish to be known as witches but they got that reputation because they were, in some way, different from their fellows, with some physical pecularity that set them apart from their neighbours. Human nature being what it is, we are often ill at ease with a person different from ourselves and don't always show the tolerance we should.

One thing is certain. There is still a strong belief in the supernatural even today. Do you cross your fingers when you are about to tackle a tricky problem? Do you take a 'good luck' mascot with you when sitting an exam or taking part in some kind of competition? Do you ever 'touch wood' when making an optimistic forecast? If so, you must, deep down, have a belief in something very like witchcraft. If you read 'Your fate in the Stars,' so popular in today's newspapers and magazines, then you are following in the footsteps of your witchcraft-believing ancestors. It is sad to think of how much those reputed witches must have suffered, both from the Law in the early days and from their neighbours later on after the law no longer prosecuted them. One thing, however, ought to comfort a true Yorkshire man or woman. We were a lot less cruel to our witches than they seem to have been in other parts of England and we were kindness itself compared with Scotland or the Continent where many thousands of witches suffered a cruel death.

There are no witches nowadays? Oh, but there are. Groups or covens of witches exist in North Yorkshire today. They won't, however, do you any harm and might even do you a bit of good with their activities. Modern witches tell us that they believe it is possible to harness certain powers outside themselves and use them for healing sickness and solving problems. Perhaps it would be as well to be careful, though. Witches are people after all and human nature has its weaknesses. Perhaps we ought to keep a bit of rowan wood handy, just in case. No evil spell can touch you then — at least that's what our great-great-grand-parents believed.

Index of Witches, Reputed Witches, Wise Men and Wise Women

Classified under the names of towns and villages in Yorkshire with which they are associated (geographical location of places shown on the 'witch map'). *Note*: The numbers after each name refer to page(s) in text where each is mentioned.

(anon.) = the name of witch/wise man is not known.

(?) = sources differ as to place or name of witch/wise man.

Select Bibliography

Printed material consulted:

Atkinson, J. C., 'Forty Years in a Moorland Parish,' 1891.
Blakeborough, J. Fairfax, 'Yorkshire Days and Yorkshire Ways,' 1935.
'Yorkshire Village Life, Humour and Characters,' 1977.
Blakeborough, Richard, 'Yorkshire Wit, Character, Folklore and Custom,' 1898, reprinted 1973.
'The Hand of Glory and other Grandfather's Tales,' ed. J. Fairfax Blakeborough, 1924.
Bogg, Edmund, 'Wensleydale and the Lower Valley of the Yore,' *c*.1895.
Brown, June and Crodes, Ian, 'Staithes,' 1977.
Charlton, Lionel, 'History of Whitby and Whitby Abbey,' 1779.
Crowther, Patricia, 'Witchcraft in Yorkshire,' Dalesman, 1973.
Dowson, F. W., 'Goathland in History and Folklore,' 1947.
English, Brenda, 'Five Generations of a Whitby Medical Family,' 1977.
Gee, H. L., 'Folk Tales of Yorkshire,' Nelson, 1952.
Gutch, Mrs, 'Examples of Printed Folklore concerning the North Riding of Yorkshire,' 1906.
Harrison, B. J. D. *et al*, 'Guisborough before 1900,' 1980.
Henderson, William, 'Notes on Folklore of Northern Counties and the Border,' 1866, reprinted 1973.
Hole, Christina, 'Witchcraft in Britain,' Granada, 1979.
Home, Gordon, 'Evolution of an English Town (Pickering),' 1905.
Jeffrey, Shaw, 'Whitby Lore and Legend,' 2nd ed., 1923. Repr. Caedmon Pr. 1985.
'Mother Shipton's Prophecies,' Collection of the earliest editions, 1881, reprinted 1978.
North Riding of Yorkshire Quarter Sessions Records, 1606-1657, *c*.1890, in 8 volumes, ed. J. C. Atkinson.
Ord, John Walker, 'History and Antiquities of Cleveland,' 1846.
Stonehouse, William, 'Tom Keld's Hole,' 1880.
Surtees Society, 'Depositions from the Castle of York (1640-1680),' 1861.
Yorkshire Archaeological Journal, Vol. 14, 1898.

Documents
Parish Registers of Danby, Goathland, Guisborough, Lythe, Marske-by-Sea.
Mr. B. Frank. Notes on the MSS of George Calvert's writings, which he very kindly allowed me to examine.